KU-316-538

The Complete Book of CLASSIC SAMPLE LETTERS

Sample Letters That Get Results and have stood the test of time

Compiled by Lee Jarvis

foulsham
LONDON • NEW YORK • TORONTO • SYDNEY

foulsham

The Publishing House, Bennetts Close,
Cippenham, Berkshire, SL1 5AP, England

LEEDS METROPOLITAN
UNIVERSITY
LEARNING CENTRE

1703014 80X

10B✓

P05567   21·11·00

808·066 JAR

ISBN 0-572-02262-X ✓

Copyright © 1997 W Foulsham & Co.

All rights reserved

The Copyright Act prohibits (subject to certain very limited
exceptions) the making of copies of any copyright work
or of a substantial part of such a work, including the
making of copies by photocopying or similar process.
Written permission to make a copy or copies must therefore
normally be obtained from the publisher in advance.
It is advisable also to consult the publisher if in any doubt as
to the legality of any copying which is to be undertaken.

Typeset by WestKey Ltd, Falmouth, Cornwall
Printed in Great Britain by
St Edmundsbury Press,
Bury St Edmunds, Suffolk

Contents

Introduction

We have many ways of communicating with other people. We can hold conversations, face to face, expressing our meaning by body language and facial expression and by the way we speak the words we are communicating. Or we can telephone – but then we have no means of *showing* what we mean; our meaning must be clear in what we say and how we say it. And, of course, both of these methods of communication are subject to inter-ruption and to side-tracking, so that our message gets lost or misunderstood. Passing on messages via intermediaries can lead to complete breakdowns in communication! You know the sort of thing. You ask Joan to remember to tell Mary to remind George to meet John at the bus station on Monday evening at 8 o'clock. The chances are that George will be looking for David at the railway station at 7 o'clock on Tuesday! You may have heard the age-old story of the message passed down the line: it started as 'Going to advance, send reinforcements,' and was received as 'Going to a dance, send three and fourpence'.

Most of us feel, at some time or another, that we need a foolproof way of getting our message through to someone else. We could tape-record our words; that would be a way of saying what we mean – if only we didn't get flustered in front of a microphone and "Umm" and "Aah", and forget where we've got to, and sound so boring. Or, we could – guess what! – write a letter!

A letter communicates one side of a conversation. With a little thought you can communicate *exactly* what you want to say. The person receiving your letter has a permanent record of your message, can think about it, and reply – providing the other side of the conversation. It's quite a remarkable thing, if you think about it. All you need is a pen, a piece of paper, and a postage stamp, and you can express your thoughts, your wishes, your feelings, to someone miles away within a day or a few days. Most of us look forward to receiving letters but dread answering them, and we dread, even more, writing all those one-off letters – of enquiry, invitation or complaint.

Why is this so? Many of us know what we want to communicate, but not how to write it. We fear that we have forgotten the rules of letter writing – if we ever knew them – and that we won't 'do it properly'. The truth is that there are no hard and fast rules of letter writing. There is, of course, the need to address the envelope correctly but, otherwise, letter writing is a matter of thought, consideration for the recipient, and conforming to the common courtesies of life, rather than of rules to be obeyed.

This book seeks to guide you rather than instruct you. There is guidance on the materials of letter writing, on presentation, and on expressing yourself correctly and, hence, unambiguously. Should you wish to write to persons of title in Britain, or to residents in other countries of the European Union, should you wish to propose marriage or express your condolences, you will find guidance in this book.

Series of model letters are given as samples for a wide range of situations, from personal to social and family business. So, whether you are writing to a loved one or a trading company, applying for a job or complaining to your landlord, you should find in these samples ideas that you can use or patterns that you can follow.

We wish you good, successful and happier letter writing!

How to Write Letters

This section provides the basic information you need on how to write good letters. You'll find everything from straightforward guidance on using an appropriate paper to instructions on the importance of proper presentation and clear letter construction in different situations. You can then move on to the sample letters in the second section.

1

Your Choice of Materials and Tools

Every letter you write represents *you*, so you should give some consideration to the stationery you use and to the means you choose to put your letter on to (and into) this stationery. Imagine you were going out to meet the person to whom you are writing. You would take some care with your appearance – even though the actual meeting was the important thing. You would aim at being clean and neat and your matching outfit would be chosen to suit the occasion. Your letter should reflect this image; it should be clean and neat in appearance and the paper and envelope should be of good quality and matching, as well as suitable for the content of the letter.

Writing paper and envelopes

Here are some guidelines:

*   **Quality**   You could ruin the appearance of your letter by using paper and envelope of poor quality. Your writing might smudge or 'print through' but, most of all, your letter will not give a good impression of you to the recipient. *Bond* is a good quality paper that looks good and that resists tearing and creasing. *Bank* is a flimsy paper that is useful for carbon copies. *Airmail* is a thin, lightweight paper used, as its name implies, for airmail letters (to keep down the cost of postage).

*   **Plain or fancy?**   Generally plain and not fancy. Colourful notelets or brightly coloured, deckle-edged notepaper are fine for chatty letters to close family or friends, but otherwise

11

plain, white or pastel shades are better, and the envelope should match the colour of the paper.

- **Lined or unlined?**   If your letter is typed, *always* unlined. If it is handwritten and you have problems in line spacing or staying horizontal, it is probably better to use paper with very feint lines printed on it although, for some reason, letters on lined paper do not look as nice as letters on unlined paper – do they? A useful tip is to rule up a blank sheet with heavy black lines, which you can slip under the page on which you are writing as a guide. This will 'show through' even bond paper, so that you can keep your lines well spaced and straight. And you can use it time and time again.

- **Sizes of paper**   Any business, or semi-business, letter (say, to a landlord, a society, the Inland Revenue, etc.) should, preferably, be written on the size of paper known internationally as A4. This size is 210 mm across by 297 mm up and down (that is, about 8¼ inches by 11¾ inches). The commonsense reason is that most office files are designed to take this size, so the recipient can easily keep your letter on file for further reference. If you are writing a short letter which will not be kept on file, A5 sized paper is fine. This measures 148 mm across by 210 mm up and down. It is, in fact, the size you get by folding in half a sheet of A4 paper.

- **What about folding A4 to make A5?**   If you intend to cut the sheet to make two A5 sheets, it is better to use a guillotine for this, to avoid jagged edges. If you intend to write your letter on the folded sheet, think first how many A5 sides you will use. If only one side, write on the front sheet with the fold to your left. If two sheets, continue on the right-hand sheet inside the fold. If three sheets, write your page two on the reverse of your page one and end your letter opposite, on the right-hand sheet of the fold. It is a good idea to number pages two and three if you find you have to carry over on to page four to close the letter.

- **Envelope sizes**   Ideally, your letter should not be folded more than necessary to fit its envelope. When choosing the envelope, do make sure that it is not just a tiny bit too small for your letter, because nothing looks worse than a letter which has an extra half inch fold down one side to make it fit the envelope. It is worth noting that a C4 sized envelope takes an unfolded sheet of A4 paper; a C5 sized envelope takes a once folded A4 sheet or an unfolded A5 sheet; a C6 sized envelope takes a once folded A5 sheet.

- **Other useful envelope sizes** A great deal of business correspondence is sent in envelopes which measure 110 mm by 220 mm, so suiting A4 sheets folded in three. Just a small warning! When using these envelopes, there is not a lot of spare space, so fold your letter in three as accurately as you can. Refolding can make a letter look very messy.

  Then there are the POP (Post Office Preferred) sizes, the range recommended by the Post Office so that mail up to 60 grams in weight can be electronically sorted. Within this range, envelopes should not be smaller than 90 mm by 140 mm (3½ inches by 5½ inches) and not larger than 120 mm by 235 mm (4¾ inches by 9¼ inches). You may have noticed that the C4 envelope does not come within the POP range and will, generally, have to be hand sorted by the Post Office, along with very small or large envelopes and mail weighing more than 60 grams.

- **Manilla envelopes** Although, for social letters, paper and envelopes should match, it is acceptable to use manilla envelopes with white writing paper for business letters or when an envelope of extra strength is required.

- **Window envelopes** These are frequently used for business correspondence. The addressee's name and address is written on the letter, which is then folded so that this shows through a 'window' on the front of the envelope. The difficulty in aligning the letter so that the address is clear throughout the letter's journey, is the main reason for not using such envelopes for family correspondence.

- **Airmail envelopes** When writing fairly short social letters overseas by Airmail, the simplest stationery to use is an Aerogramme from the Post Office. This gives you paper and envelope in one, with postage paid. For longer letters, you can use an Airmail envelope (made of strong, lightweight material to keep down the cost of postage) or an ordinary envelope (which may weigh more) with an Airmail 'sticker' which your Post Office will supply. For both of these you should write clearly 'LETTER' under the Airmail label and you should have the letter, in its envelope, weighed at the Post Office so that the correct postage is paid.

If you are including, say, a small gift with your letter, do check with your post office if you should complete a Customs Declaration slip. Some countries require this. The form is very simple to complete, and it could well save your letter being opened for inspection, and so delayed, when it reaches its country of destination.

The tools of letter writing

The next thing you need is something with which to write! The choices are fairly limited: pencil, crayon, pen, typewriter or word processor. Again, some guidelines:

- **Pencil or crayon**   Excellent for very young children who are being encouraged to write notes of 'Hello!', 'Thanks' etc. from an early age, but – except in very special circumstances – not for others. Exceptions for writing a letter in pencil might be because of a physical incapacity, or because the writer is confined to bed. You should not choose a pencil so that you can then rub out and change what you have written. It will certainly be a very 'tatty' letter if you do! Instead, draft your letter in pencil, altering it as you need to, and then copy it out neatly using a pen or typewriter.

- **Pen**   Use a reasonably good pen with which you feel easy and which fits comfortably in your hand. This will allow you to write as clearly as possible and without blotches and smudges. The colour of the ink should be blue or black. With a new ballpoint pen or a new cartridge of ink, try this little test before you start writing. On an odd scrap of paper, write a few words, then drip on to these a spot or two of water. Let the paper dry and examine the words you have written. Are they still clear? In other words, is the ink fixed and waterproof? If not, don't use the ink for your letter. Getting 'damp' in the post might mean your letter is quite unreadable and possibly not deliverable if the address on the envelope also 'runs'.

- **Keeping a copy** If you want to keep a copy of your handwritten letter (and it is advisable to keep a copy of any type of business letter), it is better to spend a few pence on a photocopy than to press hard when writing to get a rather spidery carbon copy.

- **Typewriter** If you have a typewriter and some ability in typing, you may find that your business letters have more authority when typed. Carbon copies are no problem, either. Social letters are, by convention, usually handwritten. However, if your handwriting is really bad and you can't improve it, it would be better to type most of your social letters (not your love letters, though; always write these by hand). Actually, the worst handwriting to decipher is often not the untidy and irregular writing, but the tiny spidery writing where the 'a's, the 'e's, the 'o's and the 'r's all look like the same tiny wriggle! It is worth checking with a close friend or relative if your writing is, in fact, clear to read, and if not, think of using a typewriter. Always type your letters in black and make sure the ribbon is in good condition before you start. Just one last point. If you have difficulty 'thinking' on a typewriter, draft your letter by hand and then copy it in type. 'Thinking' on a typewriter will come with practice.

- **Word processor** If you have access to one of these you can save yourself a great deal of time and effort and your letters will be neat and professional-looking. 'Thinking' on a word processor is little problem, since you can correct and make changes easily, even adding or deleting sentences or paragraphs if you have second thoughts. Often, the machine will have a system for checking and correcting spelling, and this can be a great help. You can produce copies when and where you want to, and they will all look like originals. This can be valuable if you need to send the same letter to several people; you can even change each copy to suit.

2

The Shape and Style of Letters

If you look carefully at family business letters you have received, you will see that there is a shape to the way in which they are presented. This makes them appear both attractive and authoritative and you, as the recipient, feel – whatever the content – that the writer is treating you with respect.

When you write your own family business letters you, too, should aim at a consistent shape, so that you make an immediate good impression on the recipient. If you can carry this 'shaping of letters' into your personal and social correspondence, your friends and family will feel just that little bit more important in your eyes *and* you will find your letters much easier to write.

The two main shapes

The first 'shape' is known, technically, as *blocked* (or *fully blocked*). Example 1 shows a letter in the blocked style.

The second 'shape' is known as *indented*. Example 2 shows the same letter in the indented style.

In this book, the model letters will be in the blocked style, but the indented style would have been equally correct. What is not acceptable is a mixture of styles within the same letter. Example 3 shows how you might shape a hand-written letter to a friend, using the blocked style.

Example 1   Blocked Style

Fairview
139 Polder Lane
SEATOWN
Kent LM5 3BN

6th March 19—

Mr R.A. Bloggs   Your ref. AZ76B
Manager
Messrs Fielding & Sons
16 High Street
PURSELY
Kent LM4 2YJ

Dear Mr Bloggs

Work on extension building at 139 Polder Lane

I am most dissatisfied with the way the work is being carried out
by your workforce on the extension building to my house.

As you will know, the agreement was that you would have the
work completed by the end of February but, to date, the electrical
wiring and plastering have not been started and the windows and
doors have not been painted.

As I explained to you when accepting your estimate for the work,
it is essential that the extension is habitable by 24th March 19— at
the absolute latest. Will you please, therefore, inform me on which
day I may expect your workers to return to complete the work
according to our agreement.

Yours sincerely

Mary Brown

Mary Brown

Example 2 Indented style

Fairview,
139 Polder Lane,
SEATOWN,
Kent LM5 3BN

6th March 19—

Mr R.A. Bloggs,   Your ref. AZ76B
Manager,
Messrs Fielding & Sons,
16 High Street,
PURSELY,
Kent LM4 2YJ

Dear Mr Bloggs,

<u>Work on extension building at 139 Polder Lane</u>

I am most dissatisfied with the way the work is being carried out by your workforce on the extension building to my house.

As you will know, the agreement was that you would have the work completed by the end of February but, to date, the electrical wiring and plastering have not been started and the windows and doors have not been painted.

As I explained to you when accepting your estimate for the work, it is essential that the extension is habitable by 24th March 19— at the absolute latest. Will you please, therefore, inform me on which day I may expect your workers to return to complete the work according to our agreement.

Yours sincerely,

Mary Brown

Mary Brown

Example 3 Blocked style – personal letter

34 Prospect Place
Fenbridge
Worthing
West Sussex
BN99 8XY

4th August 19–

Dear Jane

How very kind of you to invite us to your engagement party on 30th August. John and I will be delighted to attend; we so look forward to seeing you again and to meeting Steve.

Young Ben is thriving. Mother has now recovered from her spell in hospital, we are thankful to report, and has volunteered to baby-sit for us so that we can join you in your celebrations.

See you on the 30th then!

Love and best wishes

Annette

DETAILS OF THE LAYOUT

Take another look at Examples 1, 2 and 3. There is a basic layout which follows these guidelines:

- Sender's address: This is put in the top right corner of the first sheet of the letter. Note the difference in alignment for the two styles. The postal town and the postal code use capital letters. With a long county name, it is better to start the postal code on a new line.

    Note that, for large postal towns (e.g. Bournemouth) and cities (e.g. London, Bristol), and those that give their name to counties (e.g. Gloucester), the county is not written.
- The date: One line space is left below the address and then the date is written. It should start in alignment with the first line of the sender's address, in both styles.
- The recipient's address: You won't need to include this for personal correspondence. Otherwise, leave one line space under the date and move across to the left side of the page, where you write the name, title and address of the person to whom you are sending the letter. With both the blocked and the indented style this address is aligned with the left-hand margin of the letter. (If you have used a separate line for the postal code in your own address, use a separate line for the recipient's postal code – for consistency.)
- References: For business correspondence (to guide the recipient in finding the file of previous correspondence). These are normally written, on separate lines, beginning opposite the first line of the recipient's address and directly below the date.
- The opening greeting: Leave a line space and begin 'Dear Sir', or whatever is the appropriate opening for the person to whom you are writing, at the left-hand margin.
- Heading: Again, useful for business correspondence since the recipient can see, immediately, the subject of the letter. A line space is left under the opening greeting and the heading starts at the left-hand margin for the blocked style, or is centred for the indented style. In either case it should be underlined.

- The main text: Notice the styles in the Example letters, with a line space after the heading and between paragraphs. If you are using the indented style, make all the paragraph indents the same.
- The complimentary close: Leave a line space after the main text of the letter and, depending on which style is used, position the complimentary close as indicated in the Example letters.
- The signature: This is signed, by hand, directly below the complimentary close. Because so many signatures are difficult to decipher, it is helpful in any sort of business correspondence if the writer writes his or her name, very clearly, underneath the signature with, if appropriate, his or her job title or position.

The use of punctuation

You may have noticed in the three Example letters that, although they all use normal punctuation for the main text of the letters, those in the Blocked style do not use commas at the ends of lines of the addresses. There are reasons for this.

Firstly, commas seem to suit the Indented style, that is, the traditional style, whereas the Blocked style, the more modern style, looks neater without commas. Secondly, as you will read in Chapter 3, the Post Office asks us to address our envelopes for delivery in the UK without any punctuation. This helps with electronic sorting. If there are no commas in the address on the letter, this will better match that on the envelope. However, it is a matter for your own preference.

Here are some points for your guidance in the use (or not) of full stops:

- Whichever style you choose, there should be *no* full stop after: the post code; the date; the heading; or the writer's name and job title at the end of a letter.
- Where words are contracted so that the last letter of the word and the last letter of the contraction are the same, there is no full stop after the contraction. For example, Rd (Road) and Mr (Mister).

- Where words are abbreviated so that the last letter of the word and the last letter of the abbreviation differ, there *is* a full stop (except, of course, on the envelope; see above and Chapter 3). For example, Esq. (Esquire) and ref. (reference).
- The letters used to abbreviate a person's given names have full stops after them (again, but not on the envelope).
- It is becoming more and more common *not* to use full stops between the letters of a person's awards, honours and degrees. This seems very reasonable. A string of letters can look very 'spotty' if all the full stops are used, and the letters can be very difficult to group.

Note

There is more guidance on addresses in Chapter 3.

3

Opening and Closing Letters, and Addressing Envelopes

Opening greetings

Conventionally, many letters open with the word 'Dear'. This should not be taken as a term of affection. Here are some opening greetings you are likely to come across and use, yourselves:

- Dear Sir or Dear Madam
  These are the customary openings for business correspondence.
- Sir or Madam
  Sometimes used in business correspondence, these openings are more formal. When used for family business they could suggest a certain curtness on the writer's part, so think carefully before using these openings, yourself.
- Dear Sirs
  This is the correct opening when your letter is not addressed to an individual, but to a company or to 'Messrs So and So'. For more formality, the alternative, 'Sirs' can be used in business correspondence.
- Mesdames
  This is the correct opening when writing, formally, to a group of ladies. *Never* open with 'Dear Mesdames'.
- Gentlemen or Ladies
  Used only occasionally, and with care, for great formality or when you wish to orate (as in a circular letter, for example).

(You should note that, since no names are mentioned in any of the above, you should make clear – by the way you address your letter – the individual, or the branch/department if appropriate, so that it is clear to the recipient for whom your letter is intended.)

- Dear Mr Jones or Dear Mrs Jones or Dear Miss Jones or Dear Ms Jones
  These are the correct openings when you know the person to whom you are writing or have had previous correspondence with him or her. If you don't know the marital status of a lady to whom you are writing, it is better to address her as 'Ms'. Some ladies prefer to be addressed as 'Ms' anyway.
- Dear John Jones or Dear Mary Jones
  These openings are acceptable as slightly less formal than the previous openings. On the whole, most people would prefer to be greeted 'Dear John' or 'Dear Mr Jones', depending on how well they are acquainted with the writer. So, use the 'Dear John Jones' form of greeting sparingly.
- Dear Tom or My Dear Tom
  These openings are used between friends and relations, in both family business and personal correspondence. In such cases (and when you write 'Dear Mum', for example), the recipient does perceive an affectionate implication in the word 'Dear', so use the form 'My Dear' very sparingly.
- My Darling Tom or My Dearest Mary
  These openings are for special cases of affection and, obviously, are never used in any form of business correspondence.

The complimentary close

This is the term used for the way in which a letter is, conventionally, ended. Here, the word 'complimentary' is used in the sense of 'fulfilling the duties of courtesy'. Here are some ways of closing your letters, correctly and courteously:

- Yours faithfully
  This is the form generally used for business letters when the recipient is not named in the opening greeting (for example, when 'Dear Sir', 'Dear Madam', 'Dear Sirs' is used. *Never* write 'Yours very faithfully'.

- Yours sincerely or Yours very sincerely
  These are used for business letters where the recipient is greeted by name (for example, 'Dear Mr Jones', 'Dear John Jones'). The 'very sincerely' form can be used to suggest a more friendly feeling towards the recipient. (Note that it is acceptable to qualify 'sincerely' by 'very' but, as stated, 'faithful' cannot be qualified in this way. One is either faithful or not faithful!)
- Best wishes (followed by) Yours sincerely
  This is a more friendly way of ending a business letter when the recipient is greeted by name and is well known to the writer. It can also be used for certain social letters.
- Faithfully yours or Sincerely yours
  These endings are used only rarely since they can seem a little pompous.
- Yours respectfully
  This ending should *not* be used for family correspondence since it can seem very servile. Conventionally, the ending is used for a long letter in the form of a report.
- Your obedient servant
  This form is used only in certain official letters. (It is a conventional ending for such letters and should not be taken literally!)
- Yours affectionately
  Suitable for relations, would-be relations and between girlfriends.
- Yours ever or Love
  Used only when writing to a close friend.

Addressing envelopes

The address on the envelope gives the recipient a first impression of you. If it is clear and well laid out, the impression will be favourable; if it is unclear and messy, it may never arrive, let alone impress the receiver.

Start addressing the envelope about halfway down and towards the middle. The name of the person to whom the letter is addressed goes in the first line and the address follows in lines beneath, using the blocked style (that is, the left-hand side should *not* be indented). If your letter includes the recipient's address, this same address should be used on the envelope, but with one important variation:

- Because much of the inland mail is now sorted electronically, the Post Office asks us to omit any punctuation (and this includes the full stops after abbreviations) since addresses without full stops and commas are easier for the automatic machinery to read.

If you now look back at Examples 1 and 2 on pages 18 and 19, you will see that the correct way of addressing the envelope for both of these is:

Mr R A Bloggs
Manager
Messrs Fielding & Sons
16 High Street
PURSELY
Kent LM4 2YJ

And, if you now look at the hand-written letter, Example 3 on page 20, the correct way of addressing this envelope would be:

Miss Jane Hanson
Glen Cottage
Straight Road
GLOUCESTER
GL2 8LM

MORE EXAMPLES OF ADDRESSING ENVELOPES

Here are some more examples, together with guidance notes:

Mr L E Brown   John Adams Esq
Willow End   Flat 15
Country Rd   147 George Street
ASHTONE   BRISTOL
Devon PL9 4AB   BS19 2XY

Notes

* Inverted commas should not be used for the names of houses, e.g. as for Willow End, above.
* Esq. (or Esq on the envelope) and Mr are *alternate* forms used for addressing men and they must never be used together. If the first name or initials are not known, use 'Mr Adams', never 'Adams Esq.'.

• • • • •

The Revd James Smith
The Rectory
Church Lane
BOTWICH
Lancs LA7 2EF

Dr and Mrs Stephen Jones
16 Dunkley Avenue
ASCOT
Berkshire
SL9 2KL

Notes

* The Revd is the abbreviation of 'The Reverend' and has no full stop. An alternative form is 'The Rev.', a contraction which, hence, takes a full stop (but not on the envelope). Using either form, the Christian name, or at least the initials, should precede the surname. If the letter is sent on a church matter, it would be courteous to add a line under the name, such as 'Rector of St Botolph'.
* Counties such as Lancashire (Lancs), Berkshire (Berks) etc., that can be abbreviated, may be written in either form. Even though these are not true contractions, a full stop should not be used after the county.
* When writing to a doctor, it is safer to use 'Dr' rather than to address him as Stephen Jones MD, or Stephen Jones Esq. MD, unless you are absolutely certain that 'MD' *is* the correct doctorate. Mrs Jones should be included as shown, unless she is also a doctor, in which case the correct form would be 'Doctors Stephen and Sylvia Jones'.

• • • • •

Mr Tom Williams and
Ms Tessa Hopkins
9B Carter Court
BRIDGFORD
Hants GU8 3BB

Mrs Jane Robinson
10 Yeadon Rd
LLANPENAU
Gwynedd
LL82 9FG

Notes

*   When two people of the opposite sex are cohabiting, there is often a problem of how to address a letter to both of them without causing embarrassment. It may be that Tessa and Tom are married but that Tessa chooses to continue using her maiden name. In such a situation, the address above is correct. If you are not sure of their marital state, or of their wishes, the sensible thing to do is to ask them how they prefer to be addressed. If this is not practical, the safest thing to do is to address the envelope to 'Mr Tom Williams', but to make it clear that the letter is to both of them by opening with 'Dear Tessa and Tom', for example.

*   It has been customary in the past to address Jane as 'Mrs Paul Robinson' or 'Mrs P. Robinson' if her husband, Paul, was still alive. The form 'Mrs Jane Robinson' would have been the correct way to address her, only if she were widowed. Nowadays, however, many women prefer to be addressed by their own given name and, indeed, this is sensible when business or social correspondence concerns them as individuals.

*   There is no need to write 'Wales' or 'North Wales' after the county (Gwynedd). The post code will establish the location. Similarly, for your letters to Scotland and Northern Ireland.

•   •   •   •   •

Special Note

** When you are sending letters or postcards to the UK from overseas, you should write the country (ENGLAND, SCOTLAND, WALES or NORTHERN IRELAND) clearly at the end of the address.

A tip from experience! If you are posting cards or letters to Wales, Scotland or Northern Ireland, from foreign post offices well away from the normal commercial or tourist centres, you might do well (provided this won't upset the recipients!) to write (ENGLAND) or (via ENGLAND) at the bottom of the addresses. It will help with the sorting and your correspondence will not be delayed or misdirected. There is a greater probability that the sorter will know 'ENGLAND' rather than 'WALES' etc., or even 'UK'.

4

How to Address Persons of Title

Should you write a letter to a person of title in the UK, there are certain conventions that you should follow in addressing the person and in the opening greeting and the complimentary close. You are not obliged to follow these conventions, but it is courteous to do so.

HM THE QUEEN
Address Her Majesty the Queen
Begin: Madam   *or*   May it please Your Majesty
End: I have the honour to remain (*or* to be), Madam
          Your Majesty's most humble and obedient
          subject

ROYAL PRINCES
Address: His Royal Highness
          The Prince of –
Begin: Sir
End: I have the honour to remain (*or* to be), Sir
          Your Royal Highness's most humble and obedient
          servant

ROYAL PRINCESSES
Address Her Royal Highness
         The Princess of –
Begin: Madam
End: I have the honour to remain (*or* to be), Madam
         Your Royal Highness's most humble and obedient
         servant

DUKE
Address His Grace The Duke of –
Begin: My Lord Duke
End: Yours faithfully

DUCHESS
Address Her Grace The Duchess of –
Begin: Dear Madam
End: Yours faithfully

MARQUESS, EARL, VISCOUNT, BARON (Peers, other than
a Duke)
Address The Most Hon. The Marquess of –
         The Rt Hon. The Earl of –
         The Rt Hon. The Viscount –
         The Rt Hon. The Lord –
Begin: My Lord
End: Yours faithfully

WIFE OF A PEER
The wife of a Marquess is a MARCHIONESS
The wife of an Earl is a COUNTESS
The wife of a Viscount is a VISCOUNTESS
The wife of a Baron is a BARONESS

Address The Most Hon. The Marchioness of –
         The Rt Hon. The Countess of –
         The Rt Hon. The Viscountess –
         The Rt Hon. The Lady –
Begin: Dear Madam
End: Yours faithfully

BARONET
Address Sir (Christian or given name and surname), Bt
Begin   Dear Sir
End: Yours faithfully

BARONET'S WIFE
Address Lady (Surname only)
Begin: Dear Madam
End: Yours faithfully

KNIGHT
Address Sir (Christian or given name and surname), with the
appropriate letters after his name
Begin: Dear Sir
End: Yours faithfully

KNIGHT'S WIFE
Address Lady (Surname only)
Begin: Dear Madam
End: Yours faithfully

ARCHBISHOP (of Canterbury or York)
Address The Most Reverend and Rt Hon. The Lord
         Archbishop of –
Begin: My Lord Archbishop
End: Yours faithfully

BISHOP
Address The Right Reverend The Lord Bishop of –
Begin: My Lord Bishop
End: Yours faithfully

DEAN
Address The Very Reverend The Dean of –
Begin: Dear Dean
End: Yours sincerely

ARCHDEACON
Address The Venerable The Archdeacon of –
Begin: Dear Archdeacon
End: Yours sincerely

AMBASSADOR
Address His Excellency (followed by style, title or rank and
         Christian or given name and surname)
Begin: My Lord *or* Sir (according to rank)
End: I have the honour to be, My Lord *or* Sir (according
         to rank)
         Your Excellency's obedient servant

MEMBER OF HER MAJESTY'S GOVERNMENT
Address A letter sent to a Minister as the head of his/her
         department is addressed by his/her appointment only.
Begin: Dear Sir *or* Madam
End: Yours faithfully

If the writer knows the Minister concerned, it is permissible to
greet him or her by the appointment, for example:
Begin: Dear Prime Minister
         Dear Lord Privy Seal
         Dear Chancellor
End: Yours sincerely

LORD MAYOR
Address The Rt Hon. The Lord Mayor of –
Begin: My Lord Mayor
End: Yours faithfully

MAYOR OF A CITY
Address The Right Worshipful The Mayor of –
Begin: Mr Mayor (whether male or female)
End: Yours faithfully

MEMBER OF PARLIAMENT OR EUROPEAN PARLIAMENT
As in private life, according to rank, with the addition of the
letters MP or MEP after the name and any awards. As
examples:
Mr A.R. White OBE, MP *or* A.R. White Esq., OBE, MP
Mrs J.A. Black MEP *or* Mrs Joan Black MEP

• • • • •

Should you wish to write to persons of title not given in this
chapter, there are several books on the correct etiquette when
addressing such persons. Your Librarian will be able to advise
you.

5

Letters to 'Europe'

This chapter gives some guidelines on the courtesies and conventions that you should use when writing to other countries of the European Union. Although, at present, most of us think of 'Writing to Europe' in terms of pen-pal letters, hotel bookings, thank you letters, and the like, it is probable that, in the near future, we may need to write directly to, say, companies about some products, rather than through an agent in Britain.

The first general, but very important guideline is:

- Unless you are completely literate in the language of the person to whom you are writing, do not 'have a go' at that language in your letter. For any other than pen-pal letters, efforts using phrase books and dictionaries will be at best hilarious and at worst incomprehensible. (We've all chuckled at such as, 'Please confirm that our room has large widows' and 'Please describe your modern conveniences', so we should be well aware of the hazards!)

- There are two alternatives. The first is to write in English and hope that the recipient will understand your letter or will get it translated. The second is for you to have your letter written into the language of the recipient by a professional translation service.

- Whichever method you decide on, try to keep your letter brief and to the point.

Opening and closing letters, and addressing envelopes

If you are having your letter translated, the opening and closing and the envelope address will be put into the correct form by the translator. However, if you are writing in English, there are some courtesies and some conventions you should follow.

What you should *not* do, is mix styles, *except* for titles. For example, 'Dear Mr Verdi' or 'Dear Signor Verdi' are correct openings when writing, in English, to Italy. 'Egregio Signor Verdi', whilst correct if the letter is in Italian, is better avoided when your letter is in English.

However, the address on the envelope is a different matter. Never try to translate a foreign address into English; here you must 'mix styles' or it's very likely your letter will not be delivered. For example, if Mr Verdi lives in 'Via Bianco', it is not likely that he will receive a letter addressed to him in 'White Street'!

The section that follows gives you guidance and examples on how to open and close letters and address envelopes, for the different languages of the countries of the European Union.

DANISH

For letters to Denmark.

Opening greeting:	Dear Mr / Mrs / Miss Hansen or Dear Sir / Madam / Sirs
Complimentary close:	Yours sincerely / Yours faithfully
Envelope address:	Mr (or Hr) Bernhard Hansen Sankt Anna Plads 5 DK-1250 KØBENHAVN K Denmark

Notes
It is courteous to write the given name, not just the initial. When writing to a lady, the envelope address would be, for example, Mrs or Miss (or Fr) Britta Hansen.

DUTCH

For letters to The Netherlands and to the Flemish-speaking regions of Belgium.

Opening greeting: Dear Mr / Mrs / Miss Rinckes
                            or Dear Sir / Madam / Sirs

Complimentary
close: Yours sincerely / Yours sincerely /
                  Yours faithfully

Envelope address: Mr (or De Heer) A Rinckes
                            Directeur
                            Bekaert Netherland NV
                            Kasanyelaan 53
                            DEN HAAG
                            Netherlands

Notes
It is customary to use just the initial, not the full given name. When writing to a lady, the name is of the form Mrs (or Mevrouw) N Rinckes or Miss (or Mejuffrouw) N Rinckes.

ENGLISH

For letters to the UK and to the Republic of Ireland. (See Chapter 3)

Note
When addressing the envelope, the country is The Republic of Ireland (not 'Ireland' and not 'Eire').

FINNISH

For letters to Finnish-speaking persons of Finland. (Finland has two official languages, Finnish and Swedish.)

Opening greeting: Dear Mr / Mrs / Miss Metsä
                            or Dear Sir / Madam / Sirs

Complimentary close:	Yours sincerely / Yours faithfully

Envelope address: Mr (or Hra) Matti Metsä
                       Aallonkohina 8 D 77
                       (SF-)00130 HELSINKI
                       Finland

Notes
Either the first given name or the initials may be used. When writing to a lady, the name is of the form Mrs (or Rouva) Kaarina Metsä or Miss (or Neiti) Kaarina Metsä.

FRENCH

For letters to France and to the French-speaking regions of Belgium and Luxembourg.

Opening greeting: Dear Mr / Mrs / Miss Pierron
                       or Dear Sir / Madam / Sirs

Complimentary
close: Yours sincerely / Yours faithfully

Envelope address: Mr (or Monsieur) Paul Pierron
                       29 rue de Missine
                       F-75017 PARIS
                       France

Notes
It is courteous to write the first given name when this is known. When writing to a lady, the name is of the form Mrs (or Madame) Marie Pierron or Miss (or Mademoiselle) Marie Pierron. The abbreviations M for Monsieur, Mme for Madame, and Mlle for Mademoiselle, are acceptable.

GERMAN

For letters to Germany, Austria, and to the German-speaking regions of Belgium and Luxembourg.

Opening greeting:	Dear Mr / Mrs / Miss Becker or Dear Sir / Madam / Sirs
Complimentary close:	Yours sincerely / Yours faithfully
Envelope address:	Mr (or Herrn) Hans Becker Parkstrasse 42 D-2000 HAMBURG 62 Germany

Notes

Either the first given name or the initials may be used. When writing to a lady, the name is of the form Mrs (or Frau) Inge Becker or Miss (or Fräulein) Inge Becker. It is customary to address unmarried ladies of mature age as Frau, not Fräulein.

GREEK

For letters to Greece.

Opening greeting:	Dear Mr / Mrs / Miss Skendros or Dear Sir / Madam / Sirs
Complimentary close:	Yours sincerely / Yours faithfully
Envelope address:	Mr (or Kov) P Skendros 6 Constantinou Street 109 10 ATHENS Greece

Notes

Either the first given name or the initials may be used. When writing to a lady, the name is of the form Mrs (or Ka) M Skendros.

If you have your letter translated into Greek, you will probably find that the Greek alphabet has been used. Do make sure that the country (Greece) is also written in English on the envelope, to avoid sorting difficulties in this country.

ITALIAN

For letters to Italy.

Opening greeting:	Dear Mr / Mrs / Miss Verdi or Dear Sir / Madam / Sirs
Complimentary close:	Yours sincerely / Yours faithfully
Envelope address:	Mr (or Egr Sig) G Verdi Via Testi 36 20126 MILANO Italy

Notes

It is customary to abbreviate titles on the envelope (for example Egr Sig, for Egregio Signor), but not in the letter. The first given name or the initials may be used.

It is customary in Italy for titles such as 'Engineer', 'Doctor', 'Professor', etc. to be used rather more generally than we would use them. It is a courtesy to address people by the title that they normally use.

When writing to ladies, this also applies. If no other titles are used, the form should be Mrs (or Gentile Signora) A Verdi or Miss (or Gentile Signorina) A Verdi. An unmarried lady of mature years should be addressed 'Mrs' or 'Gentile Signora'.

PORTUGUESE

For letters to Portugal.

Opening greeting:	Dear Mr Eduardo Lopo Dear Mrs / Miss Maria Coimbra Lopo or Dear Sir / Madam / Sirs
Complimentary close:	Yours sincerely / Yours faithfully
Envelope address:	Exm° Senhor Eduardo Lopo Av da Liberdade 126 1398 LISBOA Portugal

Notes

It is courteous to use all the given or fore names in the opening greeting and on the envelope. Ladies may choose whether to take their husbands' surnames or not; in any case, they will retain their own family names.

When writing to ladies the form used is Mrs (or Exm^a Senhora D) Maria Coimbra Lopo.

SWEDISH

For letters to Sweden and to Swedish-speaking persons of Finland.

Opening greeting:	Dear Mr / Mrs / Miss Evensson or Dear Sir / Madam / Sirs
Complimentary close:	Yours sincerely / Yours faithfully
Envelope address:	Mr (or Hr) Stephan Evensson Nybrokajen 9 S - 111 39 STOCKHOLM Sweden

Notes

Either the first given name or the initials may be used. When writing to a lady, the name is of the form Mrs or Miss (or Fr) Gertrud Evensson.

SPANISH

For letters to Spain.

Opening greeting:	Dear Mr / Mrs / Miss Labordo or Dear Sir / Madam / Sirs
Complimentary close:	Yours sincerely / Yours faithfully
Envelope address:	Mr (or Sr D) Carlos Labordo Salvador Av Meridiana 273 BARCELONA - 11 Spain

Notes

It is courteous to use the first given name and the two surnames on the envelope. Normally, Spanish people have two surnames; the first of these is used for the opening greetings, but both should appear on the envelope.

When writing to ladies the form used is Mrs (or Sra Doña) Maria Labordo Salvador or Miss (or Srta) Maria Labordo Salvador.

·   ·   ·   ·   ·

If you would like more details than are outlined above, or if you wish to write to overseas countries not within the European Union, we suggest you refer to *A Secretary's Handbook: Addressing Overseas Business Letters*, by Derek Allen and published by W Foulsham. Indeed, we acknowledge to that book for much of the information outlined here.

Just a final guideline! Do take note of the way in which people from overseas write to you. Copy down their addresses as given in their letters and keep a record of how they give their own names.

6

Constructing Letters

Content

Before you start your letter, take a moment or two for thought. Even in chatty letters to family and friends, there will be a few 'I must remember to tell them' aspects that you will want to include rather than add on as a string of PSs. So, jot down all the points you need to get across and put them in some sort of order, before you start your letter.

A basic structure for a letter should be that, as far as possible, you are communicating one main point or idea in each paragraph and, if the letter is intended primarily to communicate a very important point, this point should be apparent in the first paragraph. If you think about letters you have received, you will realise how annoying it is to have to skip through a page or two of rambling thoughts before coming to the *reason* for the letter – whether it be to tell you Mary is getting married, George wants to borrow some money, or that you'll have to wait for a month before the spare part you need is available.

If your letter is any sort of a business letter, ordering and structuring is of great importance. Generally, the recipient will not have time to try to work out what you are attempting to communicate. This must be clear on a first read-through. And do remember to be polite and courteous.

One final point. Even with letters to close friends, *never* write anything that might be construed as libellous; you could well regret this at some time in the future. If you must pass on scandal or unkind thoughts, it is better to do this face to face in conversation.

Grammar

The gap between what we get away with in speech and what is correct in writing is a major problem to many would-be letter writers. The rules of English grammar may seem very complicated, but they have been established to ensure that the written message communicates with the reader and does not confuse or cause misunderstanding.

Fortunately, the average letter writer doesn't need to be an expert in the rules of grammar. All that is needed is a familiarity with the structure of correct sentences and proper spelling and punctuation. If you know how to write and punctuate a sentence correctly, and if you avoid writing long and complicated sentences, your reader will receive the message you intend, clearly.

You may care to 'dip into' the rest of this chapter to find the guidance you may need on sentence construction, grammatical pitfalls to avoid, punctuation and spelling.

The sentence

The sentence is a group of words that makes complete sense. To make complete sense it must contain a subject (a word or words about which the sentence says something) and a predicate (a word or words about the subject). As a simple example: 'The boy ate an apple.' is a sentence. 'The boy' is the subject and 'ate an apple' is the predicate.

GUIDELINES

- You should avoid splitting the subject and the predicate. Do not write:
    David, after hitting John in the playground, apologised.
  Write, instead:
    After hitting John in the playground, David apologised.
- You should avoid splitting infinitives (to run, to speak etc.). Do not write:
    Peter wanted to carefully and meticulously clean the family car.

Write, instead:
  Peter wanted to clean the family car carefully and
  meticulously.
- You should not change the subject within a sentence.
  Do not write:
  We were cold on the beach because one felt the wind.
  Write, instead:
  We were cold on the beach because we felt the wind.
- You should not change the tense in your sentence.
  Do not write:
  Jane answered the telephone but nobody speaks.
  Write, instead:
  Jane answered the telephone but nobody spoke.

SOME GRAMMATICAL PITFALLS

Collective nouns

Collective nouns are nouns which are singular in form but refer
to a group of persons or things. You must be careful to use a
singular or plural verb depending on the purpose of the par-
ticular sentence.

  The committee was furious with the plans for a strike.
(That is, the committee was acting as a group.)

  The committee were arguing among themselves over the
  plans for a strike.
(That is, the committee were obviously acting as individuals,
not as a unit.)

Pronouns and adjectives

The most common error involving pronouns is in phrases using
'me' and 'I'. For example, 'between you and I' is wrong and
should be 'between you and me'.

Another error is in the use of 'myself'.
It is correct to write:
  'I washed myself' and 'I don't believe that, myself'.

It is not correct to write:

My wife and myself watched the film.

Write, instead:

My wife and I saw the film.

Similar to the problem of the collective noun is the problem of 'distributive' adjectives and pronouns. These are: anybody, nobody, everybody, either, neither, each, every, none. They are all singular, and must be used with verbs or pronouns in the singular.

Do not write:

Everybody who travels abroad must have their passports.

Write, instead:

Everybody who travels abroad must have his or her passport.

And, do not write:

Each of the children were given balloons after the party.

Write, instead:

Each of the children was given a balloon after the party.

Verbs

Verbs are singular or plural depending on the singular or plural nature of their subject.

It is correct to write, either:

Those dishes, left over from Julie's party, have not been washed.

Or:

That stack of dishes, left over from Julie's party, has not been washed.

The use of 'and' is like the plus sign in mathematics and makes a plural total. For example:

John and Kathy were at the restaurant.

If we use any other words to join John and Kathy, this does not happen.

John, as well as his girlfriend Kathy, was at the restaurant.

Adverbs

The most common mistake here is to use an adjective when an adverb is required.
Do not write:
   She ate the biscuits very quick.
Write, instead:
   She ate the biscuits very quickly.

Prepositions

Avoid using the prepositional phrase 'due to' when 'because of' conveys the correct idea.
Do not write:
   The cricket match was stopped due to the rain.
Write, instead:
   The cricket match was stopped because of the rain.

Avoid using the verb 'following' when prepositions and pre-positional phrases such as 'after', 'because of', 'as a result of', and 'in accordance with', are more accurate.
Do not write:
   Following the heavy rains, the roads flooded.
Write, instead:
   Because of the heavy rains, the roads flooded.
Or:
   After the heavy rains, the roads flooded.

Miscellaneous errors

The use of 'than'.
Do not write:
   John is cleverer than me.
This is incorrect because the complete sentence would be:
   John is cleverer than I am.
Write, instead:
   John is cleverer than I.

The use of 'less' and 'fewer'.
'Fewer' should be used when the persons or objects can be counted.

Use 'less' when what is referred to is a quantity or an amount.
Write:

> James ate no fewer than four biscuits at tea.
>
> James takes less sugar in his tea than I do.

Punctuation

The most commonly used punctuation marks in English are:

full stop	.
colon	:
semicolon	;
comma	,
parentheses	( )
question mark	?
exclamation mark	!
quotation marks	"
apostrophe	'

Full stop

Every declarative sentence must end with a full stop.

Colon

The colon signals that an explanation or more information follows.

It is used to introduce a series.

> The child wanted three things for Christmas: a large stuffed animal, some coloured paper, and a small bicycle.

It is used to introduce a quotation, usually a rather lengthy one.

> My mother's favourite saying is from Mark Twain: "Work consists of whatever a body is obliged to do . . . Play consists of whatever a body is not obliged to do."

It is used to separate two clauses of equal weight.

> Paul said it was time for supper: I said we had just finished lunch.

Semicolon

This functions mainly in a long sentence to separate clauses where a pause greater than a comma and less than a full stop is needed.

Comma

The comma is the most frequently used punctuation mark.

It is used to separate items in a list of three or more words.

It is used to separate phrases which depend on the same word.
   I have travelled in Canada in a canoe, in Egypt on a camel, and in England on a train.

It is used in a long sentence when a natural pause occurs.

Parentheses (sometimes known as brackets)

These are used in pairs when the writer has an interruption or aside not necessarily relevant to the main idea of the sentence. Sometimes dashes are used instead of parentheses.

Question mark

This is used at the end of a sentence that is a direct question.
   Is there any milk on the doorstep?

Do not use for an indirect question.
   Mother asked if there was any milk on the doorstep.

Exclamation mark

This is used at the end of a sentence when a strong feeling is present. A single exclamation mark is enough.

Quotation marks

These are used in pairs to enclose direct quotations.
     He asked, "Where is my umbrella?"

Apostrophe

The apostrophe is used to indicate an omission as in won't, can't or it's. You should note a common pitfall here. It's means it is; the apostrophe must *never* be used with its in the possessive form (meaning belonging to it).

The apostrophe is, however, used to show possession in other cases.
     This is Mary's hat. (singular)
     Where are the boy's clothes? (singular boy)
     Where are the boys' clothes? (plural; more than one boy)

But, as stated above:
     Here is its cover.

Capital letters

You should use an initial capital letter:

- to begin a new sentence
- to begin a full quotation
- to indicate proper nouns or adjectives (England, Englishman)
- for the names and titles of people and the names of companies, books, films, newspapers, etc.
- to name specific courses (A level)
- for the days of the week and the months.

You should *not* use a capital letter for the seasons of the year or for general classes (for example: He wants to be president, but, he is President Clinton).

7

Phrases and Words

Phrases to avoid

You should always try to avoid using slang expressions and euphemisms in your letters. The very good reason is that the person receiving may not understand the expression or, perhaps worse, misunderstand it.

You should also avoid using clichés. Even though many of the family business letters we receive are full of these, we should not use them if a simpler phrase can be used instead. Here are a few 'old faithfuls', together with alternatives that you might use, instead.

Avoid	Use instead
At this moment in time	Now
At your earliest convenience	As soon as possible
We are desirous of	We would like
Your goodself	You
Furnish particulars	Give details
Owing to unforeseen circumstances	Unexpectedly
Enclosed herewith	I enclose
inst, prox, ult	(Give the name of the month)
Re your letter	With reference to your letter
In the course of	During
A considerable period	A long time
Consequent upon	After
Due to the fact that	Because
In the event of	If

In the near future   Soon
On the question of   About
With the object of   To

Words to avoid

If you can, avoid words with which you are not familiar. When you have to use an unfamiliar word, make sure you know its meaning and that you are using it correctly. You should also give thought to whether the person to whom you are sending a letter will understand unfamiliar words, and understand them correctly. Here are a few words that might not be generally familiar, and alternatives you might use, instead.

Avoid	Use instead
accomplish	do
acquiesce	agree
acquire	get, gain
anticipate	expect
approximately	about
ascertain	find out
currently	now
despatch	send
endeavour	try
facilitate	make easier
locality	place
majority	most
materialise	take place
proximity	near
remunerate	pay, reward
terminate	end
utilise	use

If you are in any doubt at all about the meaning of a word you intend to write in your letter, do check it in your dictionary.

Spelling

It is worthwhile to keep a dictionary close by when you write your letters. Even simple words that you use in conversation every day can be a problem when you come to write them down. Take, for example, your sister's daughter: is she your 'neice' or your 'niece'?

A simple jingle to help you with 'ie' and 'ei' words is as follows.

I before E, when sounded as E, except after C,
Or when sounded as A, as in neighbour and weigh.

There are so many rules and exceptions to rules in spelling that the most useful advice that can be offered here is: if you are in any doubt at all, check your dictionary – and then try to remember the correct spelling for the next time you need to write the word.

The section that follows will help you to check your spelling of words that are, commonly, spelt incorrectly.

SPELLING CHECK

Commonly misspelt words

abbreviate
absence (noun), absent (adjective)
access, accessible
accept
accidentally
accommodate/accommodation
acknowledge
acquaint/acquaintance
acquire
across
address
advertise (never -ize)
advice (noun), advise (verb) (never -ize)
affect (mainly a verb),
  effect (mainly a noun)
aggravate
agreeable
allusion
amateur
amount

anonymous
answer
anxiety
apology/apologise (or -ize)
apparent
appearance
appreciate/appreciation
architect/architecture
assess
attach
autumn

bachelor
baring
barring
basically
bear
beautiful/beautifully
beginner/beginning
belief (noun), believe (verb)
beneficial/benefited
bolder (adjective)
bore/boring
boulder (noun)
breadth
Britain (the country), Briton (inhabitant of Britain)
Britannia
British
Brittany (in France)
brochure
budgeted
bulletin
bureau (plural bureaux/bureaus)
bureaucracy/bureaucratic
business

calendar
capital (city or letter)
category
ceiling
cemetery

colleague
college
commemorate
commitment
committed/committing
committee
comparative
compatible
competence
competitive
complement (that which completes)
compliment (to pay a . . .)
compromise (never -ize)
conference
connection
connoisseur
conscience
conscientious
conscious
consensus
convenience
correspondence/correspondent
corroborate
courteous
courtesy
curriculum/curriculum vitae

deceive
decide/decision/decisive
deficient
definite/definitely
deliberate
dependant (noun), dependent (adjective)
dilemma
disappear
disappoint
disapprove
discipline
discreet (prudent)
discrete (separate)
discrepancy

dissatisfied
dissimilar
dissolve
distributor
dyeing (colouring)
dying (death)

eighth
embarrass/embarrassment
enquire (to ask)/inquire (more
  detailed investigation)
enrol/enrolment/enrolled/
  enrolling
emigrate
equipment
equipped
especially
etc. (etcetera)
exaggeration/exaggerated
excellent
excerpt
excise (never -ize)
exciting
exercise (never -ize)
exhaust/exhausted/exhaustion
exhibit/exhibition
experience
extraordinary
extremely

favourite
February
financial
finish
foreign/foreigner
formally (strictly)
formerly (previous)
forth (forward)
forty
fourth (4th)
fulfil/fulfilled/fulfilment

gauge
government
grammar
grateful
grievance
guarantee
guard

handkerchief (plural handkerchiefs)
harassment
height
honour/honourable/honorary
humour/humorous
hygiene/hygienic
hypocrisy
hypothesis (plural hypotheses)

illusion (deceptive appearance)
immediately
immigrant
imminent
improvise (never -ize)
incidentally
incipient
independent (noun or adjective)
indispensable
influential
install/installation/instalment
intelligence
irrelevant
irreparable
irresistible

jeweller/jewellery
judgement/judgment
judicial
jury/juror

knickers
knowledge/knowledgeable
knuckle

language
launderette
leisure
liaison
licence (noun), license (verb)
lose/losing
loose (adjective)
lying

maintenance
manage/manageable
manoeuvre
marriage
Mediterranean
messenger
miner (mine worker)
minor (small)
ministry
miscellaneous
mortgage

necessary
negotiable
neither
niece
ninth
noticeable
nuisance

occasionally
occupation/occupy
occur/occurrence/occurring
offence (noun), offensive
  (adjective or noun)
omit/omitted (verb), omission (noun)
opponent

paid
panic/panicking
parallel/paralleled/paralleling
parliament/parliamentary

passenger
permanent
permissible
persevere
personal (adjective)
personnel (noun – staff or employees)
persuade
picnic/picnicking
piece
planning
possess/possessive/possession
potential
practice (noun), practise (verb)
precede/preceding/predecessor
preference/preferred
preliminary
preparation
prestige
principal (most important)
principle (basis)
privilege
probably
procedure
profession/professional
professor
profit/profitable/profited/
profitability
pronounce/pronunciation
pursue

questionnaire

realise (or -ize)
receipt
receive
recognise (or -ize)
recommend/recommendation
reference
refer/referred/referral
repetition
resign/resignation

satisfactory
schedule
scheme
sensible
sentence
separate
similar/similarity/similarly
sincerely
sing/singing
singe/singeing
skilful
solicitor
specialise (or -ize)
stationary (still)
stationery (paper)
statutory
subtle/subtlety
succeed/success/succession/
successful/successfully
suddenness
supersede
supplement
suppress
sympathy/sympathetic

tariff
technical
temporary
thorough
transfer/transference/transferred
Tuesday
twelfth

unconscious
undoubtedly
unfortunately
unnecessary
until
useful/useless
usual/usually
utensil

vehicle
veranda/verandah
vermilion
versatile/versatility
vertebra (plural vertebrae)
veteran
veterinary
vie/vying
view/viewing
vouch/voucher

warehouse
weather (wind, rain, etc.)
whether ('whether or not')
Wednesday
withhold
wool/woollen/woolly

zero (plural zeros)
zoo/zoological

You may care to pencil in the correct spellings of other words that you have problems with, alongside those that have been listed.

Sample Letters

These sample letters will guide you in your own family letter writing. They are grouped under broad headings and there is a list of all the letters, and where you can locate each of them, at the end of the book.

Should a letter exactly suit your needs, please feel free to copy it – but do remember to change names, dates etc. Otherwise, we hope that the samples will give you help with how to present your own letters. If nothing more, they could give you ideas on that all too familiar sticking point – how to start.

You may notice that the sample letters are free from 'slang' and 'euphemisms'. Although we use these in conversation, we should not use them in letter writing for the simple reason that they may not be understood by the recipient.

Please note

- Generally, the sender's address and the date have been omitted in these samples. You should, of course, include your address and the date in your own letters.

- The addresses that are given in the samples are invented, as are the names of people, companies, products etc.

- Signatures have been omitted in these samples. You should, of course, sign your letters by hand, directly below the complimentary close.

8

Job Applications

Whether you are applying for your first job or for a new job, the letter of application that you write could well be the most important letter you ever write; on it could hinge the rest of your life!

Remember that your letter will be one amongst dozens – maybe hundreds – that the prospective employer will receive. It will be your ambassador and will be an important deciding factor as to whether or not you are included in the employer's short list of applicants.

Your letter must be typed, or neatly hand written, and should include all the relevant information but *not* unnecessary details. Think, clearly, what you want to say before you start your letter, and then write truthfully and without clichés and pompous language.

Your CV

The object of a CV (curriculum vitae) is to present an outline of you – your education, your previous employment and your personal status. It is normal to include the names of two referees, but do make sure these persons are willing to supply references if asked.

Your CV should state the facts. It should be clearly displayed on a separate sheet and enclosed with your letter. Two examples are given here to guide you. There are professional agencies who will prepare your CV for you if you are nervous about preparing your own.

1 Curriculum vitae (1)

Name: Jane Brown

Address: 43 Chalcot Park
             London NW1 6AX

Telephone: home 0171 485 0396

Date of birth: October 7th 1978

Marital status: single

Secondary education: St Mark's School
                       Edgware
                       Middlesex TP4 3SZ
                       1990–1994
                       5 CSEs English Language (C)
                               Mathematics (C)
                               Geography (D)
                               Art (E)
                               English Literature (E)

Job experience: Temporary clerical work with Jones Bros Ltd, Tower Road, London N1 2ER, August 1993 and 1994.

Referees: Mr S Collins
             Office Manager
             Jones Bros Ltd
             Tower Road
             London N1 2ER

             Mrs R Smith
             Headmistress
             St Mark's School
             Edgware
             Middlesex TP4 3SZ

You may choose not to disclose your marital status to a prospective employer. As legislation stands at the time of writing, employers must not take marital status into account when selecting staff.

2 Curriculum vitae (2)

Name: John Smith

Address: 69 Lower Terrace
              Onsworth
              Bedfordshire DB7 2SJ

Telephone: home Onsworth 638006
              office Onsworth 534662

Date of birth: 8th August 1948

Marital status: married

Education since 11   Penworthy Grammar School
                       Penworthy
                       Bedfordshire FT2 6PN
                       1959–66
                       6 'O' levels
                       3 'A' levels   History Grade B
                                         Geography Grade C
                                         Latin Grade C

                       Worth University, 1966–69

                       BA (History) Second Class Hons

Employment: Management Trainee with Unitech Limited, Unitech
              House, Queen St, Onsworth DB6 6TZ, 1970–71;
              promoted to Assistant Manager (sales) 1971–75;
Present position: Area Manager (marketing) with Framley (UK) Ltd,
              Thorpe Way, Onsworth DB2 2PT (since 1975).

Referees: Mr K Park
              Faculty of Arts
              Worth University
              Worth FP6 2NP

              Mr B Crane
              Managing Director
              Framley (UK) Ltd
              Thorpe Way
              Onsworth DB2 2PT

3 Job application – with CV

(address and date)

The Personnel Officer
ABC Ltd
36–41 Hope Road
London EC3 7YP

Dear Sir

I wish to apply for the position as Sales Representative (Europe) which was advertised in today's *Daily News*.

I have had nine years' experience of the type of selling you outline, starting as a trainee with CDE Ltd, and progressing to my present position of Area Sales Representative (Home Counties) with LMN Brothers of Croydon. I am now keen to advance my career with a larger organisation which offers opportunities to sell in Europe.

I enclose my curriculum vitae, in which you will see that I am fluent and literate in the French language and that I have a good working knowledge of German.

If you consider that I am a suitable applicant for your advertised position, I should be happy to attend an interview where I could give you further details.

Yours faithfully

Colin Parks

Enc.

It is as well to use the contracted form 'Enc.' to indicate that there is an enclosure (in this case, your CV) with the letter.

4 Job application – without CV

(address and date)

Ms Joan Brady
Office Manager
Messrs F Sims & Sons Ltd
Central Road
Northtown
Berks SL3 1XX

Dear Ms Brady

I write in answer to your advertisement for a Senior Clerical
Officer in last Friday's *Evening Post*.

I am thirty years of age, unmarried and in good health. I was
educated at St Anne's Convent, Northtown, where I obtained four
GCE 'O' levels in English Language, History, Geography and
Mathematics. I then went to Northtown Polytechnic where I took a
course in office procedures and business methods.

After various temporary posts, I secured a position as Junior
Clerical Officer at Smith & Jones Limited, York Way, Northey,
where I stayed for ten years. During that time I was promoted to
Senior Ledger Clerk, a post I held until the firm was closed last
year. I am now doing temporary work again, but am very anxious
to find secure employment, and I hope you will look favourably
on my application.

I would be able to come for an interview at any time, but would
much appreciate three days' notice for the convenience of the
agency whose books I am currently on. I can provide excellent
references should you so wish.

Yours sincerely

Caroline Brown

Very often, newspaper advertisements ask applicants to write to, say, the Office Manager, Joan Brady. Never write without using the courtesy Ms/Mrs/Miss title. You could telephone the company to enquire how the lady prefers to be addressed, or use the 'safe' Ms title.

Applications 'on spec.'

As with any other job application, an enquiry written 'on spec.' must create a good impression on its reader. You will naturally speak of your own abilities, qualifications and experience, but it is also important to say in what way you think you could be useful to the reader's organisation.

If you would be willing and able to do various jobs, make this clear; but never try to impress by claiming to be able to do things which you cannot in fact manage. Say what jobs you really think you can handle, and at what level.

It is a good plan to find out all you can about the organisation to which you are writing, and then to use what you have discovered in your letter in order to show that you are genuinely interested, not just trying for 'any job'. If possible, find out the name of the personnel officer or staff manager, and write to him or her in person.

---

5 Application 'on spec.' for a position as junior shop assistant

(address and date)

J Bloggs, Music Ltd.
5 Queen's Crescent
Brimton
Bedfordshire AB4 PQ8

Dear Sirs

I wish to enquire if you expect to have a vacancy for a junior shop assistant in the near future.

I left King Edward's School last July, having passed GCSE
Examinations in English Language, Music, Geography and French,
all at Grade C. In my last year at school I also took a course in
typing and general office procedures.

I have been playing the piano for some years and hope to pass at
Grade 6 in a month's time. I have also just started flute lessons. I
play keyboard and sing with the local group, *Splash*.

Since leaving school I have not been able to find a regular job, but
I have done some temporary work with Messrs Smith and Jones,
who have been pleased with my work. Mr Smith has himself
assured me that he will be quite willing to give me a favourable
reference.

I realise that you may not have any vacancies at present, but I
would be very willing to work in any way connected with music,
and to undertake any training required. I therefore hope that you
will consider my application favourably should a position arise.

Yours faithfully

Karen Jones (Miss)

---

6 Application 'on spec.' for a job in a garage

(address and date)

Mr H Bloggs
Director
Brownlea Garage
Poulford
Lancs MN4 3CK

Dear Mr Bloggs

Please would you consider employing me in your garage?

I am 17 years old and left school last year with good grades, as
you will see from my CV.

Your mechanic, Mr Fred Black, mentioned to me that your business was expanding and that you were expecting to take on a new agency in a month or two. Mr Black is a neighbour and a friend of my family. As such, he has taught me a great deal about the workings of cars and their proper maintenance.

During school holidays I have helped out at several local garages, including Brownlea Garage, mainly vacuuming customers' cars. I am happy to take on any routine jobs to start with, just to work with motor vehicles.

I should be pleased to attend for an interview at any time should you consider my application favourably.

Yours sincerely

Stephen Green

Enc.

---

7 Application 'on spec.' for a position in a sales department

(address and date)

K Crane Esq.
Personnel Officer
Maplock (UK) Limited
Maplock House
Lower Road
London W6X 5PJ

Dear Mr Crane

I wish to enquire if you may have a vacancy, at an executive level, in your Sales Department. James Brown, who is a mutual acquaintance, suggested that I write to you because he tells me that your firm is expanding in this area just now.

As you will see from the enclosed curriculum vitae, I have a sound educational background, and several years' experience in the sales departments of two well known firms. Whilst employed with Tailor Marketing I also gained valuable experience as a salesman 'on the road'.

You may have heard that my present employers, Thorpe & Co. Ltd, are closing down at the end of September, and it is for this reason that I shall be made redundant next month. I am very anxious not to remain without work for long, and am quite willing to consider any post for which you think I may be suitable and where I could be of service to your company.

Yours sincerely

John Bone

Enc.

Always tell the people whom you are naming as referees, even if you are quite certain that they will not mind.

---

8 Asking someone to give you a reference

(address and date)

M Deacon Esq.
Timber Products Limited
Poolford
Dorset YT7 9IJ

Dear Mr Deacon

I am applying for the post of Works Manager at the Royal Oak Timber Company, Markyate, and wonder whether you would allow me to give your name as a referee.

Although I have always been very happy working at Timber Products, my wife and I would like to move nearer to her family now that our baby is on the way.

If my application is not successful, I hope that you will not feel I am in any way dissatisfied with my job here. The move would be entirely for family reasons.

Yours sincerely

James Long

---

9 Following up a reference (from a prospective employer)

(address and date)

Mrs B Brown
The Cedars
Love Lane
Porton
Hants SH1 5BB

Dear Mrs Brown

Miss Emily Jordan, of 25 Oakley Avenue, Milton, has applied to me for the post of Cook to my family. I understand that she was employed by you for some years in a similar capacity. She has given your name as a referee and I would be grateful if you could let me know if you found her capable and totally reliable.

Whatever you write will, of course, be treated in complete confidence. I enclose a stamped addressed envelope.

Yours sincerely

Mary George

Writing a favourable reference is quite easy. If, however, you feel you cannot recommend the person, it is best to refuse the reference, politely.

10 Reference letter

(address and date)

Mrs Mary George
The Oaks
23 Briggs Road
Chelton
Hants SH6 9LL

Dear Mrs George

In reply to your request for information about Emily Jordan, who
has applied to you for the position of Cook, I confirm that she
worked for me for four years as Cook to my large family.

I always found her honest and reliable. As to her capability, she
was a very good plain cook but not very ambitious in her menus.
That suited us very well. If that is what your family requires, I
think you will find Emily an excellent choice.

If you would like further information, please contact me again.

Yours sincerely

Betty Brown

It is advisable to mark letters of reference 'Confidential'. If your
reference includes any reservations you should include these,
but never write specific accusations. For example, in the letter
above, the writer has implied that Emily is not a *Cordon Bleu*
cook, but in a pleasant and positive way.

11 Reply to an invitation to attend an interview

(address and date)

J George Esq.
Kingley Marketing
64 King Street
Milton
Northants SY7 8PL

Dear Mr George

Thank you very much for your letter of 13th May. I would be happy to come for an interview on 21st May at 2.00 pm, and will bring with me the references you request.

Yours sincerely

Brian Butts

It is important to send a letter in this situation, not merely as confirmation that you will attend, but also to show that you are taking the matter seriously and paying attention to detail.

12 Accepting an offer of employment

(address and date)

R Burns Esq.
Personnel Manager
Timetec Limited
Rose Estate
Oxridge
Bucks SL9 5RF

Dear Mr Burns

Thank you for your letter of 12th October offering me the post of Ledger Clerk with your organisation.

I am delighted to accept the position and look forward to starting work with you on 15th November.

Yours sincerely

Jane Allcock

---

13 Resignation letter

(address and date)

M Broad Esq.
Personnel Manager
Flight and Pearce Limited
Malford
Berks YO9 3PM

Dear Mr Broad

I have to inform you that I have been offered the position of Chief Buyer with Smith and Allsopp of 19 High Street, and I have accepted the post since it will give me greater responsibility and an increased salary. I wish, therefore, to tender my resignation as from 31st July.

I would like to take this opportunity to say how much I have enjoyed working at Flight and Pearce. Nevertheless, I feel that I owe it to myself and my family to further my career by making this move, and would like to thank you for giving me the training and experience which have made such a promotion possible.

Yours sincerely

Simon Jones

9

Invitations and Replies

The most important thing to remember when you are sending an invitation, formal or informal, written, typed or printed, is to give the time, date and place, the type of event and your own name.

Formal invitations suggest formal events, but to make a formal invitation more personal for family and close friends, you can add a few friendly words if you wish.

14 Wedding invitation (formal)

Mr and Mrs John Fowler

request the pleasure of
the company of

(write the name of the guest(s))
at the marriage of their daughter
Marjorie
to
Mr Robert Blake

at Saint Fellows Church
Ringway
on Saturday 29th May
at 2.45 pm
and afterwards at a reception at
The Bullbrook Inn, Ringway

RSVP
21 Drum Lane
Ringway
Somerset PS9 4TJ

OR

Mr and Mrs John Fowler
request the pleasure of your company
at the marriage of their daughter
Marjorie
to
Mr Robert Blake
etc.

If the number of guests is quite low, the invitations may be written by hand on suitable attractive stationery. Usually, however, they are printed. The traditional colour for the lettering is black. Write in the name of the guest or guests clearly and neatly by hand.

RSVP means 'please reply', from the French 'répondez s'il vous plaît'.

OR

The exact wording depends on who is issuing the invitation and their relationship to the bride. For example, if the bride's parents are divorced and her mother has remarried, the wording could be:

Mr and Mrs William Stevens
request the pleasure of
the company of

(*write in the name of the guest(s)*)
at the marriage of her
daughter
June Smith
etc.

Although the bride's surname is rarely included in the wording, it can be appropriate where it differs from that of the host and hostess.

15 Reply to a wedding invitation (formal)

Mr and Mrs Peter Faulkener thank Mr and Mrs John Fowler for their kind invitation to their daughter's wedding, and to the reception. They will be most happy to attend.

OR

. . . They much regret that a prior engagement prevents them from attending.

It is usual to reply to invitations – to say whether or not you will attend – in the same style as the invitation. A handwritten reply is quite acceptable.

It is not necessary to give your full address when the reply is in the form of a brief note, so long as you establish who you are. The envelope should be addressed to whoever sends the invitation (that is, Mr and Mrs John Fowler in this example).

16 Wedding invitation (informal) (1)

Sandra and Paul Jones, Christopher and Jane

Sheila and Andrew hope you will join them, to celebrate their wedding at Saint Peter's Church, Hazletown, on Saturday 16th August at 2.30 pm and at a reception afterwards at the King's Hotel, Hazletown.

RSVP
197 High Street
Hazletown
Surrey GU88 4AB

It is a good idea to indicate clearly, as above, if children are included in the invitation. Informal invitations can be neatly handwritten or typed, or produced on a word processor, with the names of those invited handwritten to make the invitations more personal. Avoid photocopies! These can appear very impersonal.

17 Wedding invitation (informal) (2)

Auntie Jane and Uncle Reg

Andrew and I hope very much that you will come to our wedding at Saint Peter's Church, Hazletown, on Saturday 16th August at 2.30 pm. The reception will be at the Two Drakes Restaurant in Low Street. Please let us know if you will be able to come.

In the evening we are holding a disco at The Three Bears in Willowville, starting at about 8 pm. Do join us!

Love from

Sheila

It is always nice to invite older guests to dances and discos. Probably they will enjoy themselves immensely and they are very likely still young at heart.

18 Reply to a wedding invitation (informal) (1)

Sheila and Andrew

Thank you very much for inviting us to the wedding and reception on 16th August. We shall be delighted to attend. It is kind of you to include the children in your invitation. However they are at an 'awkward' age and have decided they want to go to Gran's on your wedding day. As they are never quiet for two minutes together, I'm sure they have made the right decision.

Sandra and Paul Basset

19 Reply to a wedding invitation (informal) (2)

Dear Sheila and Andrew

How kind of you to invite us to your wedding. We shall be very pleased to attend, and to come to the reception.

Uncle Reg says he's never been invited to a disco before and wouldn't miss it for worlds. He says he can still remember how to 'Twist'.

We send you both all our love and good wishes.

Auntie Jane and Uncle Reg

20 Engagement party invitation (formal)

14 Cedars Close
Littlerow
Surrey MT4 1DL

Mr and Mrs John Finch
request the pleasure of
the company of

(write in the name of the guest(s))
at an evening party
on Saturday 14th July
at 8.30 pm
at the above address to
celebrate the engagement of their daughter
Marianne
to
Mr Wayne Burton

RSVP

An invitation such as this would usually be printed. If the party is to be at a hotel or other premises, give that address in the main part of the invitation, and the home address at the bottom left, under RSVP.

---

21 Reply to an invitation to an engagement party (formal)

(address)

Mr and Mrs Peter Palmer have great pleasure in accepting Mr and Mrs John Finch's invitation for Saturday, 14th July.

OR

Mr and Mrs Peter Palmer wish to thank Mr and Mrs John Finch for their kind invitation for (to their daughter's engagement party on) Saturday 14th July, but very much regret that they will be unable to attend.

---

22 Engagement party invitation (informal)

Margaret and Peter Palmer

Marianne and Wayne have great pleasure in inviting you to their engagement party (OR hope you'll join them at their engagement party) at the Green Lees Hotel, Littlerow, on Saturday 4th July at 8.30 pm.

RSVP
14 Cedars Close
Littlerow
Surrey MT4 1DL

This invitation may be written by hand and set out as shown, or printed, with the layout in a central position as for a formal invitation.

---

23 Reply to an invitation to an engagement party (informal)

Marianne and Wayne

Thank you very much for inviting us to your engagement party on 24th July. Of course we shall be delighted to attend.

Margaret and Peter Palmer
The Tudors
Littlerow

24 Christening invitation

(address and date)

Dear Sharon

John Andrew will be christened at St Michael's Church on Sunday 30th April and Mark and I would love you to be there.

The christening is at 3.30 pm, and there is a little celebration at home afterwards. If you could arrive here between 2.30 and 3.00 pm, that would be perfect.

I do hope you will be able to come.

Love

Lindsay

25 Reply to an invitation to a christening

(address and date)

Dear Lindsay

Thank you so much for inviting me to John Andrew's christening on Sunday. I wouldn't miss it for anything.

I should arrive by 3.00 pm, but if I am delayed, don't wait, I'll go straight to St Michael's.

Looking forward to seeing you and Mark again, and of course, the baby.

Love from

Sharon

OR

Dear Lindsay

I do hope you will forgive me when I tell you that I will not be able to make the christening on Sunday.

I am going on holiday in two days' time to Florida, and cannot change the booking now.

It was very kind of you to ask me. You know I would have loved to have been there.

Expect a postcard from America. I'll be thinking of you.

Love to John Andrew.

Sharon

26 Children's party invitation

(address and date)

Dear Mrs Buckley

Samantha and Stephen are having a few of their friends to a party here on Friday 17th March, and hope that Tim will be able to come. The party is after school, between 4.30 and 8.00 pm, and is to celebrate Stephen's 8th birthday.

We shall, of course, drive any of the children home who are not being collected from the party. If, however, you would like to fetch Tim yourself, it would be nice if you could arrive at about 7.00 pm, in time for some of the fun. We would be very pleased to see you.

Yours sincerely

Debbie Brown

If the two mothers are well acquainted, first names only will be used. Although many children's party invitations are sent using pre-printed invitation cards, a letter can establish two very important things. The first is that a birthday is involved so a small gift might be in order, and the second is that the children will be taken home after the party if they are not collected by a certain time.

27 Reply to an invitation to a children's party

(address and date)

Dear Mrs Brown

Thank you very much for inviting Tim to the party on 17th March. He is really looking forward to it.

I will call in at about 7.00 pm as you suggest, to lend a willing hand and to take Tim home. I hope we'll have time for a chat.

Yours sincerely

Lyn Buckley

OR

Tim is most upset that he will be unable to come to the party on 17th March. We are driving to Scotland that weekend for my parents' wedding anniversary celebrations.

It was so kind of you to invite Tim. Will you please tell Samantha and Stephen how sorry he is to have to say 'No'.

Yours sincerely

Lyn Buckley

---

28 Thanks from a child after a party

(address and date)

Dear Mrs Brown

Thank you for the lovely party last Friday. I had a really good time and the food was super. The games were super too.

From Tim Buckley

It is a good idea to encourage children to write their own thank you letters. You may need to guide them as to what to say, but let them use their own words. Similarly, children should always be encouraged to write their own thank you letters for gifts received.

---

29 Thanks from a child for a gift

(address and date)

Dear Tim

Thank you for coming to our party. It was a good party, wasn't it? Thank you for the book about animals. I like it very much.

Stephen

10

Love and Marriage

When you write a love letter, be yourself. Write as you would talk, or would like to talk, with your loved one. And, keep at the back of your mind the thought that love letters are often treasured for many years, read and re-read.

The normal conventions for beginning and ending letters do not apply for love letters. Although *Dearest James, Darling Sandra*, or simply *Darling* are often used, originality – when it's not merely being clever – is half the charm of a love letter. Similarly with the ending. You can hardly leave out the word love altogether, but the exact wording is entirely up to you.

It is, however, best not to overdo endearments such as kisses or hearts, or they will lose their value. Do not put Xs or cryptic messages on the backs of envelopes. Whoever receives the letter will probably not thank you for letting everyone, including the postman, know about the relationship.

The letters that follow can only show one style of writing a love, or family, letter. If they sound 'wrong' to you, don't use them. At best, they are merely a framework for your own personal sentiments. You may, or may not, wish to give your address at the top of your letter. It is probably a good idea to write in the date.

30 Love letter from a young man

(date)

Darling Paula

It seems weeks since we were together, but it's only three whole days. I hope you haven't forgotten me! I love you!

I'll phone you on Thursday evening because I know your Mum and Dad will be out and you'll be able to tell me you love me without them overhearing.

I'm counting the days to our holiday together. Ten whole days in the sun with you will be heaven. Somehow we'll find a spot to get away from everybody, my love.

Take lots of care of yourself and write soon, please.

From your own

Mike

---

31 Reply, from a young woman, to a love letter

(date)

My dearest Mike

It was wonderful to get your letter. I miss you so much! It was lovely talking to you on Thursday but it's not the same as being with you, is it?

I hope all is going well with the job. Perhaps the next job will be nearer home. I do hope so. I'm so thrilled that you got the job, but I do long for us to be together again.

I'll be at the station to meet your train. I know we'll only have a few hours but they will be wonderful hours, won't they, my love?

Phone soon. I love you.

Paula

During the Gulf War, it was reported that many servicemen and their girlfriends or families at home found themselves in the position of having to write letters (there being at the time no telephone link) for the first time. They found this method of communicating without an immediate response, very difficult to cope with.

---

32 Love letter from a serviceman who is posted overseas

(date)

Ann Darling

It seems forever since I was with you, instead of three long months. If only I could phone. I long for the sound of your voice. Do you miss me as much as I miss you?

I won't say I wish you were here with me, because it's not such a good place to be. Still, we all hope and pray things will soon get sorted out and we can – as they say in the films – 'get the hell out of here'.

It was great to get your letter telling me all about your Christmas. Thanks for calling in on Mum and Dad; I heard from Mum the other day and she said how happy they were to see you and – as she always does – asked when we were going to get married and give her some grandchildren!

All things considered, we had a good Christmas out here. Plenty to eat and drink and our parcels from home turned up in good time. A thousand thanks for the sweater. It fits perfectly and is quite beautiful. You must have been knitting away every evening since we parted.

Well, my love, another letter comes to an end. You know all the things I want to say to you, don't you? Perhaps it won't be too long now. Write back soon, won't you? I need your letters so much.

All my love, now and always

Terry

---

33 Love letter to a serviceman who is posted overseas

(address and date)

Dearest Terry

It was so good to hear from you. Yes, love, I miss you too – more than you could imagine.

All of us at home send our love and we hope that you and the lads can keep cheerful. We saw a TV report about the area you are in and saw all the snow. I'm glad you liked the sweater and it fitted; I reckon you'll need it when you are off duty.

We had our first snow of the winter last week and Jane and I took her kids on to the hill for a spot of tobogganing. It was great fun, but walking on the hill brought back so many memories of us together there, last summer, that I got a bit weepy. Fingers crossed that we can go there again, together, before too long.

Jenny and all the other girls at the supermarket send their love to you. I shouldn't tell you this, but I heard they are planning to send you a stack of Valentine cards. Perhaps you'll be able to pass one or two of them to Sam and Pete, anonymously of course. I feel so sad that they have no one to write to or to hear from; it might cheer them up a bit.

I have to close now so I can catch the post. I miss you so much, and you know how much I love you. Take good care of yourself and come home to me soon. I'll write again at the weekend, when I hope I'll have had another letter from you.

My love, for ever and ever

Ann

34 Family letter from a serviceman overseas

(date)

Dear Peggy, Joanne and Wayne

Only six more months and four more days and we'll all be together again. Like you, I'm crossing off the days from the calendar.

Thanks for your last letter, Peg; I was thrilled to read that Wayne has said his first word. Are you sure it was 'Dad' he said? I hope you are managing all right, love. I wish your Mum was nearer to help you out. Still, Joanne is a great kid, isn't she; and it's good you were able to get her into playschool.

We're having mixed weather and it's quite stormy at present. We are kept hard at it, so we don't have too much time to get homesick, thank goodness. The lads are a good crowd and we try to keep the youngsters from getting too fed up. Mind you, I don't know how we'd all cope if football hadn't been invented.

There are rumours that we might get our phone line fixed this month. There will be a long queue to phone home if they get it working again, but I'll be right at the front just to have a few words and to know, for sure, that you are all well.

Write soon and let me know all the news, won't you? Give the kids a big hug from their Dad.

My love to you all

Steve

35 Reply from family to a serviceman overseas

(address and date)

Dear Steve

I had to read your last letter to Joanne four or five times. She really does miss you, and so, of course, do I.

We are all well apart from summer colds. Having a bit of time while Joanne is at playschool is a great help and I've started to decorate the bedroom. I'm enclosing a piece of the wallpaper and hope that you like what I've chosen.

Wayne can say long sentences now, and they all seem to start with 'Dad'. We haven't worked out the other words yet; Joanne says she thinks her brother is speaking in Japanese!

When Betty came round last month she took these two snaps of us in the garden. As you'll see, young Tom has a small bicycle and, of course, Joanne has been on and on at me ever since to get her one for her birthday. What do you think? I could probably find a good secondhand one and I'd make her promise she wouldn't take it out of the garden.

We all hope it won't be too long before you can phone home. Just to be able to talk together would be great, wouldn't it? Still, as Mum always says, I shouldn't have married a soldier if I couldn't cope when you went overseas.

Don't worry about us; we're all fine and we all send you all our love. Be good! Miss you and love you.

Peggy, Joanne and Wayne

36 After a quarrel, letter from a man

(address and date)

Dear Rachel

Will you forgive – and forget? Please!

I don't know how or why I could have said what I did and I am furious with myself for being such a fool.

This is the first time that we have quarrelled and please, let's make sure that it will be the last. I've never felt so miserable in my life.

When may I come round and see you again?

I love you.

John

37 Reply to a letter after a quarrel

(address and date)

Dear John

It's already forgotten. And as far as I am concerned, there's nothing to forgive. We both said things in the heat of the moment and I know we didn't mean them.

The best part of breaking up is supposed to be making up – so please come to see me soon.

I love you, too.

Rachel

38 Felicitations to a girlfriend on her engagement

(address and date)

Dearest Mary

I was so pleased to hear the news of your engagement that I just had to write to send my very best wishes – to you and of course to David. I always thought you made a lovely couple, and I am sure you will be very happy together.

Now you must come and tell me what plans you both have for the future. I'm dying to know all about them.

Love

Jean

39 Felicitations to a mother on her daughter's engagement

(address and date)

Dear Celia

May I as an old friend send my felicitations on Mary's engagement to David which I saw announced in the paper yesterday.

You must be very pleased. David and Mary seem such a suited young couple that I'm sure you need have no fears for their future happiness.

Do give my love and very best wishes to Mary.

Yours sincerely

Margaret Roberts

40 Thanks for a wedding present

(address and date)

Dear Auntie Mabel

How kind of you and Uncle James to send us such a beautiful coffee service as a wedding present. You may be sure it will see plenty of use once David and I are settled in our new home. Thank you from both of us.

We are looking forward to having you with us at the wedding. I hope you will both come to see us after the honeymoon – and find out just how good the coffee really is!

Yours affectionately

Mary

41 To an acquaintance, announcing a birth

(address and date)

Dear Mrs Almond

I am delighted to let you know that my wife, Jenny, gave birth to our first son yesterday, at Brierly Hospital. Both she and Mark (as we shall call him) are doing very well and there were no complications.

Yours sincerely

Sam White

42 To a friend, announcing a birth

(address and date)

Dear Lucy

Alan and I are so thrilled that we are now the proud parents of Mark John, who weighed in at 8 lb on Monday evening. All was well; no problems at all, and we are now back home again with Sam.

As soon as you return to Britain, do get in touch so we can drink the health of our Mark.

Love and best wishes

Jenny

43 Congratulations on a silver wedding anniversary

(address and date)

Dear Tom

It's just 25 years since I proposed a toast to a smiling groom and his lovely bride and wished them a long and happy life together.

My wishes were well founded. You and Geraldine have every right to feel pleased with yourselves. I know of only one other couple who have been as happy together as you – and you can probably guess who I mean!

Ann joins me in wishing you many more years of happiness together. We enclose a little memento of the occasion – and I hope that we shall be able to send you another one, in gold, in 25 years' time.

Yours sincerely

Chris

44 Thanks for congratulations on a silver wedding anniversary

(address and date)

Dear Chris

It was very kind of you to think of us on our silver wedding anniversary.

Geraldine and I were absolutely delighted with your letter and the lovely Wedgwood vase which is now filled with flowers and has pride of place on the dining room table.

It really was a very nice gesture indeed, and one which Geraldine and I look forward to reciprocating next year when you join us in this silvered respectability.

Our thanks and best wishes to you and Ann.

Yours sincerely

Tom

11

Clubs and Societies

Letters in this category can range from the formal to the semi-formal. If you are writing on behalf of a club or society it is wise to state, after your name, in what capacity you are acting.

45 Application to join a club

(address and date)

Mr R J Ellis
The Secretary
Frimley Gardening Club
19 Bowler Lane
Frimley
Lancs L9 4HD

Dear Mr Ellis

I wish to apply for membership of the Frimley Gardening Club.

I have been a keen gardener for many years. Mrs Brown has outlined to me the Club's activities and these sound exactly what I need to help me to be a little more adventurous!

Please send me an application form and any other information which you think may be useful.

Yours sincerely

John Ascot

Enc. 1 stamped addressed envelope.

46 Reply to an application to join a club

(address and date)

Mr J Ascot
3 Ferndale Road
Frimley
Lancs L8 9UF

Dear Mr Ascot

I enclose an application form, details of the annual subscription and this year's Club programme. The Club year runs from January to January and so your subscription for this year would be reduced proportionately.

The Club Committee considers applications for membership. Their next meeting is on 29th June. If you return the form to me in good time for this, I hope to be able to welcome you to our next meeting on 6th July.

In the meantime, you may like to make a note of our two coach trips this year to gardens of special interest. There are still a few coach seats available should you wish to join us on either, or both, visits. I shall be taking firm bookings at the July meeting. A deposit of £2 per head per visit is usual.

Yours sincerely

Ronald Ellis
Secretary
Frimley Gardening Club

Enc.

47 Requesting club subscriptions

(address and date)

To all members of the Broom Cricket Club

Dear Member

Annual Subscription

The annual subscription is due by 31st March. For the year 199- to 199- it is £20.

You may pay me at any Club meeting or, if you prefer, send a postal order or cheque made payable to 'Broom Cricket Club' to me at the above address.

Please bring or send your membership card when making this payment. A record of the payment will be written on the card.

Our 199- match schedules for Teams A and B are being finalised and we hope to send copies of the programme to all paid-up members early next month.

Yours sincerely

Tony Jackson
Treasurer

48 Pointing out an overdue subscription (formal)

(address and date)

Mr M C Brown
65 Broom Avenue
Cromer
Sussex SY7 8TR

Dear Mr Brown

Annual Subscription

According to my records, you have not yet paid this year's subscription, which became due on 31st March 199-.

The amount due is £20 and it may be remitted by postal order or cheque made payable to 'Old Cromerian's Football Club'. I would be grateful if you would give this matter your urgent attention.

Under Club rules, failure to pay by 30th June 199- will automatically result in your membership lapsing.

Yours sincerely

Frank Groom
Treasurer

49 Pointing out an overdue subscription (informal)

(address and date)

Mr MC Brown
65 Broom Avenue
Cromer
Sussex SY7 8YR

Dear Mike

Annual Subscription

Your subscription for this year is still outstanding. It would be a great help to me if you could clear this up quickly so that I can close the books for another year.

In case you have forgotten, the amount due is £20 and a postal order or cheque made payable to 'Old Cromerian's Football Club' will be gratefully received.

Please don't forget, because if your money doesn't arrive by 30th June, your membership will cease and we will have lost our best striker!

Yours sincerely

Frank Groom
Treasurer

50 Expulsion letter

(address and date)

Mr V Bourne
Flat 3
Gresham House
Gresham Street
Battley
Norfolk NO8 7JH

Dear Mr Bourne

Disciplinary Hearing

Following the disciplinary hearing which you attended yesterday, the Committee met to consider what action to take.

The complaint against you was that, allegedly, you behaved in a rowdy and abusive manner on 15th and 22nd of May and 19th June, after Club matches.

I must inform you that the Committee decided to expel you from the Club and your membership terminates today. If you have left any possessions in the Club please let me know so that we can arrange a time for you come and pick them up.

The Committee had to consider the detrimental effect your actions were having on the Club. For example, outings and fixtures were becoming increasingly difficult to arrange.

Your talent as a cricketer was praised by all and it was with reluctance, therefore, that the Committee reached its decision.

Yours sincerely
On behalf of the Battley Cricket Club Committee

Gary Hayes
Secretary

51 Advising of the formation of a society

(address and date)

Mr D Green
Butler & King Ltd
6 Carriage Road
Chorley
Essex EX5 9TR

Dear Mr Green

I write to inform you of the formation of the Greystone Court Tenants' Association. The inaugural meeting of the Association was held on 12th March, at which Mr A.G. Smith (Flat 37) was elected Chairperson, Ms FC Wheeler (Flat 28) Deputy Chairperson, and I was elected Secretary.

As the landlord's agents, I am sure your company will appreciate the greater ease of communication which this allows. I would be grateful if you would write to me on any matter concerning Greystone Court, and I will see that it is raised at the earliest possible opportunity.

Yours sincerely

James Stone
Secretary

52 Advising of an AGM

(address and date)

To all members of the
Brougham Film Club

Dear Member

Annual General Meeting

This year's AGM will be held at 8 pm on 6th April in Conference
Room H at Brougham Town Hall, 26–38 High Road, Brougham. I
enclose the agenda for this meeting and the minutes of last year's
AGM.

The AGM not only elects a new Committee, but also takes many
decisions about the Club and its activities over the forthcoming
year. I do hope, therefore, that you will be able to attend.

Yours sincerely

John Carne
Secretary

Enc.

53 Requesting a motion be put on the agenda

(address and date)

Mr F Brown
The Secretary
Dorling Social Club
41 Church Lane
London SE4 8FX

Dear Mr Brown

I am submitting the following motion for inclusion on the agenda
of the next Club meeting (21st September).

> 'This Club, recognising the heavy workload of
> the Treasurer, agrees to create the new office of
> Assistant Treasurer. The Club further agrees to elect
> an Assistant Treasurer at this meeting.'
>
> Proposer: Alan Thomas
> Seconder: Colin Reynolds

As we all know, the office of Treasurer is in danger of becoming a
full-time job. I hope that this motion, if passed, will help to
alleviate the situation.

Yours sincerely

Alan Thomas

54 Requesting club fixtures

(address and date)

Mr F Brown
The Secretary
Dorling Social Club
41 Church Lane
London SE4 8FX

Dear Mr Brown

I have recently taken on a number of new commitments and I
would like to ensure that they do not conflict with Club functions
and meetings, which I enjoy very much.

Therefore, I would be grateful if you would send me a list of the
Club's planned activities for as far ahead as possible.

Yours sincerely

Alice Ronan (Ms)

55 Reply to a request for club fixtures

(address and date)

Ms A Ronan
20 Kings Road
London SE4 3KL

Dear Ms Ronan

I enclose the Club's programme for this year. More activities may
be added and these will be notified to members at the monthly
meetings.

I am delighted that you have enjoyed the Club's functions to date.
If there are any activities missing from the list, which you would
like the Club to offer, perhaps you would inform the Committee.

We rely on suggestions and comments from members in drawing up our yearly programmes.

Yours sincerely

Frank Brown
Secretary

Enc. 1 sheet

---

56 Inviting an expert to give a talk

(address and date)

Mrs Joanne Smith-Davis
The Ashes
Bingley Avenue
Weyton
Bucks AB6 9DT

Dear Mrs Smith-Davis

The Committee and members of Weyton Lady Pensioners' Club have asked me to invite you to present your excellent talk and demonstration 'Aromatherapy' at one of our afternoon meetings.

Normally, about twenty of us meet in the Parish Hall each Friday afternoon during the summer months. We are retired professional people with a wide range of interests.

I am afraid we cannot run to offering a fee, but we are always delighted to provide transport for our speakers and to invite them to join us for lunch at The Red Lion before the meeting.

We do hope you will be able to accept our invitation. If so, please let us know a date that would be convenient.

Yours sincerely

Mollie Briggs (Mrs)
Secretary

12

Illness and Death

Sympathy letters are difficult to write. Sometimes it is better to buy a 'Get Well', or 'Sorry to learn you are ill', or 'Sympathies' card, and to add a line or two expressing your feelings. However, a letter can be of great comfort at such times, when it comes from the heart.

Such letters should be brief and to the point, without dwelling too much on the situation. Generally, they should be handwritten.

---

57 Sympathy on hearing of an illness (formal)

(address and date)

Dear Mr Wilson

We are both very sorry to learn of Mrs Wilson's illness. All of us pray that her stay in hospital will soon put things right.

Please accept our sympathies and convey our best wish for a speedy and complete recovery to your wife.

Yours sincerely

Ken and Norma Thomas

---

58 Sympathy on hearing of an illness (informal)

(address and date)

Dear Beth

Tom and I are so sorry to find that Gerald is on the sick list. We do hope it's nothing serious and that he'll soon be up and about again.

If there is anything at all that we can help you with, please give us a ring. I can easily help with shopping or fetching the children from school and Tom would gladly drive you anywhere locally in the evenings or on Saturdays.

Give our love to Gerald and tell him to get well very soon!

Kindest regards

Eve

59 Sympathy on hearing of a terminal illness

(address and date)

Dear Frank

I was much saddened to learn that your mother has been admitted to the Botstone Hospice, but relieved to know that a place could be found for her where she will have the best possible care and understanding.

I know how much you and your father have done to help your mother over these past few months and that she has your love and prayers to support her. Is there anything at all I can do to help?

I would like to visit your mother and take her some roses from the garden. They are so beautiful this year. I'll phone you at the weekend to find out what would be a suitable visiting time.

Sincerely

Tessa

Offer help only when you really mean it. With really ill people, try to find out visiting times that will not conflict with treatment etc.

---

60 Sympathy to an ill person (likely to recover)

(address and date)

Dear Beryl

I was so upset to hear that you have had to go back into hospital. I'd love to visit you, but distance forbids. However, I phoned your mother today, and she says you are making excellent progress and that you should be 'let out' by the end of next week. That's great news.

So, instead of the conventional grapes, here is a paperback to make you giggle. Don't burst any stitches though!

Best wishes for a complete recovery, very soon.

Love

Helen

---

61 Sympathy to an ill person (not likely to recover)

(address and date)

Dear Cheryl

How very sad I was to learn from your mother that you are back in hospital.

Bill and I hope that the discomfort is not too great and that you'll soon be up and about again. We know that you are getting the best possible treatment and care.

Bill has to be in London on business sometime during the next week or so and has offered to drop me off for a visit to you and to your Mum. So, see you soon and remember we are thinking of you.

All our love

Vera

Even though you know recovery is not likely, offer hope to the ill person, who may not be aware of how ill he or she is.

62 Condolences (formal)

(address and date)

Dear Mr Samson

It was with great sadness that we read the tragic news of your wife's death. We offer our sincere condolences to you and to your family; you are all very much in our thoughts.

Yours sincerely

Anna and Tony Farmer

63 Condolences (informal)

(address and date)

Dear Alice

I have just heard of your sad loss. I know that the sympathy of friends cannot lessen your grief, but I did want you to know just how much you are in my thoughts at this time.

Perhaps, in the summer, you will feel able to travel north and stay with me for a few days. I would like that very much.

My sincere condolences

Avril

64 Condolences on the death of a child

(address and date)

My dear Mary

We have just heard the tragic news. We send you and Alec, and little Ben, our deepest sympathies.

George and I just wanted you to know that you, and dear Angela, are in our prayers and in our thoughts.

Sincerely

Wendy

65 Informing someone of a relative's death

(address and date)

Dear Mr Jones

I am very sorry to have to let you know that my brother, Steve, died last Saturday. Thankfully, he died peacefully in his sleep.

He always enjoyed your chats together at the Social Club and I know you will miss him, just as we do.

The funeral will be Greenacre Crematorium at 2 pm on Thursday 19th February. We would be pleased if you would join us at the house, afterwards, for a cup of tea.

Yours sincerely

Sam Brown

66 Formal thanks for sympathies after a death

Mr and Mrs S G Brown and family are grateful for the very kind messages of sympathy which they have received.

21st February 19—

64 Green Road
Trenthurst
Northants
NH99 6AB

67 Excusing absence from work because of a relative's death

(address and date)

Mr C Smith
Personnel Officer
Crane Co. Ltd
48 Bridge Lane
Croxford
Lancs LA5 4DD

Dear Mr Smith

I regret that I was not at work today, 23rd September, and will be unable to attend for the rest of the week. My father died suddenly yesterday evening and I am needed at home to help settle his affairs and to make arrangements for the funeral. Also, all of us are very shaken by his death.

I expect to be back at work on Monday 29th September.

Yours sincerely

Carol Brown

68 From an employer in reply to the notification of the death of a relative of an employee

(address and date)

Ms C Brown
2 Creek Avenue
Forsham
Lancs LA5 9CV

Dear Carol

I was very sorry to learn of your father's death. It must have been a terrible shock for you. I sympathise with you and all your family on your bereavement.

We look forward to seeing you on 29th September, if you are able to conclude your father's affairs by then.

Yours sincerely

Craig Smith

---

69 Informing an executor of a death

(address and date)

Dear Mr Brown

I have to inform you that my father, Bernard Smith, died yesterday morning.

Since you are the executor of his will, I would be grateful if you would contact my mother or me as soon as possible, so that we can discuss the settlement of his affairs.

In case my father did not tell you, his solicitors are Groom & Sons of 19 White Lane, Whitecross, Cumbria CU6 5FG.

Yours sincerely

A Jones (Ms)

70 Notifying an insurance company of a death

(address and date)

Trust Insurance Co Ltd
69 Croft Lane
London EC1 6DR

Dear Sirs

Trust Insurance Policy No. 6781

The holder of the above policy, Gerald Young, died on 28th June. I enclose a copy of the Death Certificate.

I am executor of his will. I shall need to know the amount of money the beneficiary will receive, and when. Also, confirmation is required that the deceased's widow, Mrs Gloria Mary Young, is still the named beneficiary.

Please let me know if you need further documents before you can send me these details.

Yours faithfully

Andrew Blake

Enc.

13

Money Matters

Letters about money matters must be clear and as brief and to the point as possible. Although you may receive letters full of financial jargon, never use phrases in your own letters that neither you, nor and the person to whom you are writing, fully understand.

If you can, write to a person rather than just an organisation. If you do not know the person's name, use his/her position within the organisation. If you are not sure of the position, at least try to find the name of the appropriate department to deal with your letter.

Letters about money matters should always be polite and *never* threatening. If you feel angry, by all means communicate this feeling in your letter, but in a controlled and polite way.

Sometimes it is useful to enclose relevant documents, such as receipts. It is as well to send copies and retain the originals, making clear in your letter that this is the case.

Always quote reference numbers when you have them. This will speed up the handling of your business.

Finally, always keep a copy of any letter you write on money matters, so that you – and others involved – know exactly what has been written, to whom, and when.

INVOICES, STATEMENTS AND RECEIPTS

Invoices and Statements are issued by businesses and are prepared according to legal requirements. You may well receive these and the following examples will show you what they look like. Receipts, you may receive or need to supply yourself.

You should obtain, or provide, a signed and dated receipt for a financial transaction that you enter into privately.

---

71 Example of an invoice

Invoice No. 76   14th July 199-
To A P Smith and Sons
48 Arbroath Road
London NW8 6LR   Tax point 14th July 199-

From   Motor Traders (UK) Limited
              Bowater Street
              York SL8 9RP   VAT Regd No. 582 6543 21

Sale

Quantity	Description	Price Excluding VAT	Vat at 17½%
1	Exhaust pipe	£50	£ 8.75
2	Brackets at £10	£20	£ 3.50
		£70	£12.25
Terms: Cash discount of 5% if paid within 14 days			Total £82.25

---

72 Example of a statement

AUTO MOTORS UK LIMITED   STATEMENT
Please send payment direct to Accounts Office: 58 Ebury Street
        Manchester
Lewis Spares   LM8 6AT
6–8 West Road   Tel. 0161 898 4567
HIGH WYCOMBE
Buckinghamshire SL7 5RQ   10th February 199-

Date of sale	Reference	Amount	Reference
08/01/9-	42002 CSH	27.95	INV - invoice
15/01/9-	42069 INV	9.82	C/N - credit
21/01/9-	42098 INV	3.40	CSH - cash
05/02/9-	42121 INV	16.84	received
	Balance outstanding £2.11		

73 Example of a receipt for money received

(address)

Received from Richard Shipman, the sum of eight hundred and seventy five pounds, only, in payment for the Vauxhall van (registration number NYO 252X) delivered to him on 3rd April 199-.

(sign)

Brian Hicks
3rd April 199-

£875

74 Example of a promissory note

(address and date)

£250
Three months after date, I promise to pay Mr Fred Brown
43 Prospect Place, Birdsall RJ4 2AB, or order, the sum of
Two Hundred and Fifty pounds sterling for value received.

(Sign)

George Smithson

There may be legal requirements to stamp a promissory note.

75 Querying an invoice

(address and date)

Abbotts Stores Ltd
High Street
Mortkwith
Cumbria KW6 LM5

Dear Sirs

Invoice 2345

I have just received your invoice, dated March 6th 199-. I wish to
question the cost of the second item, Brown Boots Model AB1,
size 6. These, you have invoiced as costing £15.99. I enclose a copy
of your advertisement in the *Daily News* of February 27th 199-, in
which the cost is shown as £13.99.

I, therefore, return your invoice for amendment, please.

Yours faithfully

A. Jones (Mrs)

Enc.

76 Asking a creditor for more time to pay

(address and date)

Your ref. LN45/7896

Mr S Jefferson
16 Brockly Road
Swinton
Herts HT1 9XX

Dear Mr Jefferson

I was very distressed to receive, this morning, your letter warning
me that you intend to take legal proceedings if I do not make full
remittance of the £50 still outstanding by the end of this month.

As I explained to you by telephone, my husband has left us and
this has caused considerable financial, as well as emotional,
problems. Added to this, I learned last week that I have been
made redundant from my job as a cleaner at Matburys.

May I ask you for a little more time to pay, please. I enclose my
cheque for £10 as evidence of my wish to settle the account.

As soon as I have another job, I will send you the remaining £40.
Hopefully, this will be in the next few weeks.

Yours sincerely

Sylvia Wells

Enc.

Where you have real difficulties in repaying a debt, try to make
a realistic offer. This may well be more acceptable to your
creditor than the cost and time involved in any sort of legal
proceedings.

77 To a hire purchase company advising of difficulty in meeting repayments

(address and date)

Southern Credit Company
12–14 Arlington Street
London SW1 6HL

Dear Sirs

Agreement HP23/64/82

I am having some difficulty in meeting the repayments for the car that I am buying in accordance with the terms of the above agreement. The contract was signed on 12th August 199- and since then I have paid regularly each month. Unfortunately, because I am temporarily on short-time working, I now find that my commitments are more than my financial situation will stand.

I have no wish to default on my debt to your company. I would, therefore, much appreciate it if you would consider allowing me to make rather smaller payments over a longer period, say, a further 18 months instead of the 10 months that remain at present.

I would be most grateful if you could let me know whether such an arrangement is possible and, if so, what terms you would be able to offer.

Yours faithfully

Peter Smithson

78 Stopping payment of a cheque

(address and date)

The Manager
London and District Bank
119 Bolton Street
Royburn
Berkshire YN6 5FV

Dear Sir

Account No. 8181812 S.F. Dennis

This is to confirm my telephone call of this morning asking you to stop payment of my cheque, number 4248 638, dated 4th July 199-. It was for the sum of £586 and was signed by me in favour of Mr Eric Palfrey.

Mr Palfrey has not received the cheque and I must therefore assume that it has been lost in the post.

Yours faithfully

Simon Dennis

Only stop a cheque for a good reason, such as that it has been lost or that fraud is suspected. You will have to pay the bank for stopping a cheque.

79 Confirming the loss of a bank cheque (service) card

(address and date)

E R Cox Esq.
The Manager
London and District Bank
119 Bolton Street
Royburn
Berkshire YN6 5FV

Dear Mr Cox

Account No. 8181812 S.F. Dennis

I confirm my telephone call of this morning in which I informed a member of your staff, Miss Jones, that I had lost my Service Card, Number 456789.

I first noticed the loss this morning and I know I had it on 8th May when I withdrew money from your service till at 11 am.

Yours sincerely

Simon Dennis

80 To a shop asking why a request for hire purchase was refused

(address and date)

The Manager
Maybrick Stores
108 Pinder Street
London W1A 2AB

Dear Sir

I write to ask why I have been refused credit by your company.

I came to your shop on 18th January to buy a Hotflow 6X washing machine and a Hotflow Senior tumble drier, at a total cost of £634. Knowing from leaflets displayed within the store that you make credit facilities available to your customers, I asked for the necessary paperwork to be prepared. I was most shocked when the assistant informed me that I could not have any credit, a decision confirmed by the Department Manager, Mr Smith.

I would appreciate your explanation of this refusal, which has caused me considerable inconvenience and embarrassment.

Yours faithfully

Andrew Blackstock

Under the Consumer Credit Act, traders and finance companies are not obliged to explain why they refuse to give a person credit, but they must tell you if they have used a credit reference agency provided you ask for this information, in writing, within a month of their refusing you credit.

81 To a credit reference agency asking for your personal file

(address and date)

Black and Company
Credit House
Comley
Berkshire RP6 8SJ

Dear Sirs

I understand from Mr A. Mathews, the manager of Maybrick Stores, Pinder Street, London, that you are holding a file relating to my credit status. Since I have been refused credit by Maybrick Stores I must assume that the information you have about me, which you supplied to them, is unfavourable.

I would appreciate your sending me a copy of any information you have about my financial affairs and I enclose a postal order which, I understand, covers your handling charge.

Yours faithfully

Andrew Blackstock

Enc. 1 postal order

You are entitled by law to see and correct any files held on you by a credit reference agency, for a small handling charge. Any corrections must be passed on to anyone who has been given a reference on you in the last six months.

82 Request for an advance on a legacy

(address and date)

Mr F White   (Your ref.)
Messrs Abbott & Coles, Solicitors
193 Church Street
Toston
Devon TA7 8AY

Dear Mr White

On October 26th, you wrote to inform me of the legacy left to me by the late Miss Mary Black of Chapel View, Toston.

Since, because of illness, I am not able to work at present, I am in need of money. Would it be possible for you to advance me £500 of my legacy on account? It would help me very much.

Yours sincerely

John Jackson

---

83 Asking a solicitor to prepare a Power of Attorney document

(address and date)

Mr F White
Messrs Abbott & Coles, Solicitors
193 Church Street
Toston
Devon TA7 8AY

Dear Mr White

From 30th May 199- I shall be working in India. I expect to be travelling in that country for about a year.

Whilst I am away, I wish to give a general Power of Attorney to my brother, John Black, of 9 Rise Road, Toston, to act for me and on my behalf.

Will you please prepare the required document for my agreement and signature.

Yours sincerely

Stanley Black

Generally, for any matter more complex than drawing up a simple document, you would be advised to go and have a chat with your solicitor before writing a letter. He or she will be able to advise you on possible courses of action and the costs involved, before you commit yourself to anything in writing.

---

84 To an insurance company advising of a theft

(address and date)

Reliant Insurance Company Limited
Pimlico Street
London SW1 6XJ

Dear Sirs

Policy Number LM 169380

I have to report that a theft occurred at the above address on the night of 19th May 199-.

My wife and I were both at home on the night in question, but knew nothing of the theft until 7.30 on the morning of 20th May, when I realised that the kitchen window was open. We quickly discovered that various items were missing, and telephoned the police. I have made a full statement to the police at Banwood Police Station, where Detective Inspector Charles is in charge of the case.

I enclose a full list of the items that are missing, with their replacement values. Fortunately, nothing irreplaceable was taken and I have been able to confirm the values quite easily.

I will willingly give you any further information that may be helpful, and hope that a settlement can be made without delay.

Yours faithfully

Barry Spinks

Enc. 1 sheet

Always inform your insurance company of any claim immediately, even if you do not yet know the extent of the loss. Most companies will then send you a claim form to fill in, which would take the place of the list sent with the above letter.

---

85 To an insurance company in respect of a car accident when you believe it was your fault

(address and date)

Resteasy Insurance Company
Resteasy House
Lutton
Surrey FT5 7YB

Dear Sirs

Policy Number 685 LM 982 Z

I have to report that this afternoon, whilst driving down Maiden Vale, Lutton, I was involved in an accident with a car when I was turning right into Boundary Road. Thankfully, no one was injured.

My own car has suffered severe denting to the offside wing, which I believe will have to be replaced. The other car will require new head and side lights, a new front bumper and some repairs to the paintwork.

The driver of the other car (registration number J852 XYZ) is Mr John Bolton of 15 Harp Gardens, London, NW3 7TX. He is insured with the Kingly Insurance Company. We were not able to obtain the names of any witnesses to the accident.

I would be grateful if you could send me the necessary claim forms which I will complete and return to you as soon as I have an estimate for the repairs from my garage.

Yours faithfully

James Sudbury

Never give the go ahead for repairs to start before getting the estimate(s) approved by your insurance company. It is wise not to admit liability at this stage. You will be asked, on your claim form, to state who was responsible for the accident.

---

86 To an insurance company in respect of a car accident when you believe it was not your fault

(address and date)

Resteasy Insurance Company
Resteasy House
Lutton
Surrey FT5 7YB

Dear Sirs

Policy Number 685 LM 982 Z

I have to report that this evening, whilst I was driving down Maiden Vale, Lutton, a van overtook me and severely scraped the side of my car.

The accident was, on his own admission, entirely the fault of the other driver. His name is Ian Morton and he is an employee of Coast Deliveries (6 Oak Court, London SE16 2XN) whose van he was driving at the time.

Since no one was injured in any way, and the cause of the accident is not in dispute, the police were not called. However, a Mrs Ann Wood, of 16 Arley Road, London N8 4SP saw the incident clearly and has given me permission to mention her name should an independent witness be called for.

I have not yet obtained estimates for the repairs needed, but will forward them to you in the next few days. In the meantime, would you please send me the necessary claim forms.

Yours faithfully

James Sudbury

If an accident was not your fault, make certain you keep your no claims bonus.

14

Domestic Matters

These letters cover a wide range, from education to holidays, and from household items to house purchase.

The style and tone of your letters will depend, not only on the subject matter, but also on your relationship with the person to whom you are writing. Do remember to be as brief as possible and to keep to the facts.

Include your address and the date and any reference numbers, and write your name, clearly, under your signature. Depending on the situation, you may like to include a phone number where you can be contacted for more information or a quick reply.

---

87 Asking for a school prospectus

(address and date)

The Secretary
Peverel Hill School
Stanton
Hants SH9 8XZ

Dear Madam

Will you please send me a prospectus of Peverel Hill School.

We shall be moving to Hampshire in July, and would like our daughters, aged 12 and 14 years, to attend a suitable school as weekly boarders. Your school has been highly praised by our friends, May and John Bloggs, whose daughter, Patricia, is a pupil.

Yours faithfully

Gerald Grey

---

88 Removing a child from school because of moving house

(address and date)

C H Lovall Esq.
Headmaster
Close School
Cropston
Berks SL9 6BB

Dear Mr Lovall

I wish to inform you that our son, Neville, will be leaving Close School at the end of this term.

My husband has obtained work in Staffordshire and we shall be moving there in August.

We would like to thank you and your staff for all the help and encouragement given to Neville since he has been at Close School.

Yours sincerely

Jean Hartley (Mrs)

---

89 Requesting a child is excused religious instruction

(address and date)

Mr S Butcher
Headmaster
Berryford School
Berryford
Sussex SN3 4PD

Dear Mr Butcher

Our son Sikandar is to be a pupil at your school at the start of the winter term, and I am taking this opportunity to request that he be excused from religious instruction.

Although he was born in this country, he has been raised in the Sikh faith, and receives instruction according to our own religion.

Yours sincerely

Dilip Singh

90 Excusing homework not done (child to give letter to teacher)

(address and date)

Mr A Jones
Berryford School

Dear Mr Jones

Tommy has asked me to write to explain why he did not finish his homework over the weekend.

On Saturday afternoon, his mother presented him with a beautiful baby sister. What with all the excitement and family upheaval, I'm afraid the homework did not get finished.

I hope, on this one special occasion, you will excuse him, please.

Yours sincerely

Sam Smith

---

91 Concerning bullying at school

(address and date)

Mr P Bowlson
Headmaster
Highfield Primary School
Dean Road
Bayford
Essex EP4 1SD

Dear Mr Bowlson

Our daughter Susan came home in tears last evening. Apparently she has been the victim of a group of older girls who pick on the most junior pupils and demand money from them. When my daughter refused to hand over the little money she had with her, she was verbally abused and punched and kicked by several of these older girls.

Susan does not tell tales, and can normally look after herself, but this seems to be a particularly nasty form of bullying. She does not know the names of the girls involved except one, Karen Wilcox, who appears to be the ringleader.

As today is Friday, I am keeping Susan at home for the weekend. She is still very upset, and quite badly bruised. I intend to telephone you on Monday morning, when you will have received this letter, to seek assurances from you that this bullying will be nipped in the bud immediately and the culprits punished.

Yours sincerely

Carol Potter (Mrs)

92 Explaining a child's problem with a teacher

(address and date)

Mr P Bowlson
Headmaster
Highfield Primary School
Dean Road
Bayford
Essex EP4 1SD

Dear Mr Bowlson

Our daughter Anne seems to be experiencing a problem with one of her teachers, Mrs Woolacot.

I understand Mrs Woolacot takes Anne for science, and this has always been her weak subject. As you probably know she is very keen on most other subjects, but she does struggle at science, despite our coaxing at home.

I'm sure that Mrs Woolacot does not mean to pick on Anne but, because she is so much brighter at non-science subjects, Anne might give the mistaken impression that she is being lazy or uninterested when it comes to science.

My wife and I would like very much to visit your school and discuss this problem with you and Mrs Woolacot, in the hope that we can explain the situation, and discuss ways of assisting Anne further at home if necessary.

Both my wife and I are free to visit the school any evening after 6 pm, except Fridays.

Yours sincerely

Michael Dewhurst

93 To a carers association, requesting advice on help available

(address and date)

The Secretary
Carers Association
6 Morbridge Road
Tilton
Shropshire SH9 9ZZ

Dear Madam

Will you please send me details of your association.

My husband and I recently moved to Rigtown to care for my husband's 88-year-old father who is quite fit for his age but no longer able to take care of himself.

I have been told that there is a scheme that provides carers with an occasional few hours' relief, so that they can get away for a short time, knowing that the person for whom they are caring is well looked after. I would be grateful for information on the scheme, and for an application form so that we might join your association.

Yours faithfully

Sara Johnson

94 To an estate agent, concerning a house sale

(address and date)

Mr R Stillman
Happy Home Estate Agents
14 High Street
Brownton
Bucks AB9 4YY

Dear Mr Stillman

<u>Stanley Cottage, Bridge Lane, Brownton</u>

Following your visit, yesterday, and the advice you gave us, we would like your company to act as sole agents for the sale of the above property at an asking price of £85 000.

We agree that we will pay your commission rate of 2% plus VAT, on the sale of the property through your efforts. We accept that this rate will increase to 3% plus VAT if we decide to also instruct another Estate Agent.

We look forward to receiving, for approval, the details you are preparing for advertising the property.

Yours sincerely

Joan and John Brown

95 To solicitors, regarding the sale of a house

(address and date)

Messrs Upley, Pope and Dykes
5–7 Broad Street
Dunham
Bucks SB3 1BN

Dear Sirs

<u>32 Church Gardens, Dunham, Bucks</u>

This is to confirm our conversation of 14th May with Mrs Williams
of your office, whereby we agreed to your partnership handling
the conveyancing arrangements both for the sale of 32 Church
Gardens, Dunham, Bucks, and the purchase of New Farm, Chilton
Maltravers, Bucks. Your estimated fee was £950.00 plus VAT,
stamp duty, land registration, searches and mortgage costs.

The purchasers of 32 Church Gardens are:

> Mr and Mrs S Boyer
> 16 Berry Close
> Dunham
> Bucks SB8 5SN

The vendors of New Farm are:

> Mr and Mrs R Chapman

Please let me know what further information you require in the
form of mortgage account numbers, deeds, etc.

Yours faithfully

Robin Austin

96 Stating change of address

(present address and date)

The Manager
Central Bank Limited
4 Market Street
Hartley
Ripon RR5 4BG

Dear Sir

Accounts Numbers: P & J Nayland, 1234567; J Nayland 98765434

Please note that from 29th May 199-, our new address will be:

16 Willmore Gardens
Hartley
Ripon
RR6 7RG
(Telephone) Hartley 23186

Yours faithfully

Peter and Janet Nayland

97 Asking for an estimate for work on a house

(address and date)

Mr Tony Mitchell
T & A Windows
18 Carrow St
Muddyford
Leicester LE1 6XC

Dear Mr Mitchell

I wish to have five downstairs windows replaced by double glazed units with wooden frames. The house is old and the windows are not of standard sizes.

Your partnership's work has been recommended to me by Mrs
Black, our neighbour, for whom you did similar work last year.

Will you please come to inspect the windows and give me an
estimate. I am in most evenings and at weekends. I will need to
have the work completed by September.

Yours sincerely

Irene Grant (Mrs)

---

98 To a landlord, requesting repairs

(Address and date)

The Manager
Houselets Ltd
191 Green Road
Kingsley
Lancs LM9 3BG

Dear Sir

Flat 16B Walls Mansions, Pink Street

Will you please arrange for someone to inspect and repair the
guttering above my flat. It is badly out of alignment and rainwater
overflows down the outside walls and the windows.

The damp has now got into the brickwork and the plaster is
breaking away from the walls and ceiling in the bedroom. If this
gets worse, I feel major repairs will be necessary inside, rather
than minor repairs outside – as is now the case.

Yours faithfully

Marjorie Smith

99 Asking a landlord for release from a tenancy before the agreement has expired

(address and date)

Mr I Graham
40 Moreley Drive
Poolford
Dorset JP8 6YB

Dear Mr Graham

My husband has just accepted promotion to a new job near Bristol, and we are anxious to move into that area as soon as possible.

I realise that the tenancy agreement on the house at 94 Court Road still has three years to run, but I wonder if you would be so kind as to consider releasing us from the agreement before that time is up? If you can allow this, I would much appreciate your letting me know the date on which our tenancy could end, and the terms to which you would expect us to agree.

If at all possible we would like to leave by the end of the year and we shall, of course, be ready to consider any reasonable terms you may offer. I am very sorry to put you to this trouble, and would like to take this opportunity of saying how much we have enjoyed living here.

Yours sincerely

Irene Smith (Mrs)

100 Objecting to an application for planning permission

(address and date)

The Planning Officer
Brockford Council
Brockford Town Hall
218–240 Cross Road
Brockford
Cheshire CB4 6YZ

Dear Sir

Objection to Application for Planning Permission No. 1987

I wish to object to the proposed extension for which the above application has been made.

Having viewed the plans, I am sure that this building, if constructed, would block off the light from my lower rooms and much of my back garden during the afternoon and evening.

Therefore, I request that you reject this application.

Yours faithfully

R Hancock (Ms)

101 Circular letter suggesting a Neighbourhood Watch scheme might be set up

(address and date)

To All Residents of Chilby Road
Glimster

Dear Fellow Resident

As you will know, the number of thefts and burglaries in this area
has increased greatly during the past year. Six such cases have
been reported to the police during this month, alone. There have
also been numerous acts of vandalism on cars and on property.

It has been suggested that Chilby Road might set up a
Neighbourhood Watch scheme.

If enough residents would be willing to participate in such a
scheme, I would be willing to find out what would be involved.
We could then hold a meeting to discuss its implementation.

Would you be kind enough to complete the slip, below, and return
it to me by Saturday, 6th September, please.

Yours sincerely

Robert Leatherhead

To Robert Leatherhead
(address)

I am . . . . . .
or
I am not . . . . . .
interested in the setting up of a Chilby Road Neighbourhood
Watch scheme.

Signed . . . .

Address . . . .

102 Requesting a free sample of advertised goods

(address and date)

Castle Flooring Ltd
Dept DM 15
Queen Mary's Road
London NW6 3KT

Dear Sirs

Please send me a free sample of your 'No waste' floor covering. I enclose a stamped, self-addressed envelope.

Yours faithfully

N Chatterton

Enc.

There is no need to say in what publication you saw the advertisement. The letters and numbers in 'Dept DM 15' are the advertisers' own system of coding, telling them in which publication you read their advertisement.

103 Returning unsolicited goods

(address and date)

Crown Audio Ltd
24–30 Crewe Road
London N5 7DS

Dear Sirs

Invoice No. R978

I received a music cassette, an invoice and some order forms from you yesterday through the post. Since I neither ordered nor require this cassette, I have no intention of paying for it.

If you wish to recover this property you should write to me to arrange a mutually convenient time for someone from your company to pick it up within the next month.

Please note that I do not wish to receive any more unsolicited goods.

Yours faithfully

A G Jones

---

104 Returning unsuitable mail order goods

(address and date)

Chrome Mail Order Co. Ltd
Chrome House
19–31 Frank Road
London N22 6WK

Dear Sirs

Order No. AS536

I am returning to you the shoes (Cat. No. 83, size 5) which I ordered on 8th May and received on 23rd May. Unfortunately, on closer inspection I found that they were not exactly the colour I need.

Since I am returning these goods within the period of your money-back guarantee, I look forward to receiving a cheque for £15 from you.

Yours faithfully

A J Smith (Ms)

Enc.

---

105 To a British manufacturer, enquiring about goods

(address and date)

Customer Relations Officer
Beautiful Cutlery Ltd
Chadswick Estate
Leeds LD9 9XZ

Dear Sir

<u>Stainless steel cutlery – model ABC/123</u>

Four years ago I purchased six place settings of the above cutlery
from Kitchens Incorporated, High Street, Chegworth. These I have
found excellent, and I wish to purchase four more matching place
settings.

Kitchens Incorporated inform me that the line is now out of
production but suggest that I contact you direct, as you may hold
stocks for persons wishing to add to settings they have purchased.

Will you please advise me if you hold such stocks and, if so,
please send me a price list and order form.

Yours faithfully

B. H. Brownlow

106 To a European manufacturer, requesting parts

(address and date)

The General Director
Loppacher Segerfabrik GmbH
Marestrasse 81
D-2004 Hamburg 66
Germany

Dear Sir

Garden Hammock – D/4556A

On March 2nd 199- I bought a garden hammock made by your company from Sproggs Ltd, in London.

Two small items were not included and without them I cannot assemble the hammock as your instructions show.

Will you please send me the missing items. They are:

   1 bolt, length 3 cm (reference AB9/6)

   1 pin, length 6 cm (reference CD/8/7)

Yours faithfully

James White

Writing to an undefined 'General Director' rather than to just the company, could mean that someone with a knowledge of English is given your letter to deal with. Keep your letter brief and clear, and be sure to include any reference numbers.

107 Enquiring about holiday caravans

(address and date)

Mrs N Silver
Home Farm
Llandrew
Gwynedd LL77 5ZZ

Dear Mrs Silver

Please do you have any large caravans available on your farm for the week 7th to 14th August? Your site has been highly recommended to us by our good friends, Mr and Mrs Stevens, who stayed with you in May.

We need a caravan large enough to accommodate the two of us, our 10-year-old son, and mother-in-law. Because mother-in-law is of mature years, we would prefer a site not too far from the toilet block.

If you have a vacancy, would you please send us details and your charges for the week. We enclose a stamped addressed envelope.

Yours sincerely

Cynthia and Fred Gold

Enc.

It is courteous to enclose a stamped and addressed envelope for a reply. It is practical, too. It will probably mean you get a reply even if the accommodation is not available.

108 Confirming a holiday booking

(address and date)

The Manager
Seaview Hotel
Sea Walk
Cockle Bay
Somerset SM77 9ZZ

Dear Sir

I wish to confirm my telephone booking of 6th June. We require a double room with twin beds and private facilities, with a sea view, for six nights. We shall arrive in time for dinner on September 20th and leave after breakfast on 26th September, and will require half board.

We understand your special terms, all inclusive, will be £240 (two hundred and forty pounds) for the two of us.

I wish to pay the £60 deposit by Mastercard. The number is 3210 6543 0009 6789 and the date of validity of the card is from February 199- to January 199-.

Yours faithfully

John Palmer

109 Enquiry to a hotel in Europe

(address and date)

The Manager
Hôtel de la Poste
Villeblanc,
1009 Brussels
Belgium

Dear Sir

Thank you for your kind hospitality to us during our stay at your hotel last week. We very much enjoyed our visit and hope to return sometime next year.

Unfortunately, my wife has discovered that she has left her brown walking shoes in Room 304 of the hotel. If they have been found, she would be very grateful to have them returned to her. We would, of course, reimburse you for the costs involved.

With our best wishes

Yours faithfully

Alec Green

15

At Work

These are a few examples of letters you might wish to write in connection with your job – dealing with such aspects as absence from work, prospects, facilities, regulations, etc.

Your letters should be clear and neat. You should avoid anger. Never write anything that could reflect badly on a colleague.

---

110 Asking for unpaid leave (compassionate)

(department and date)

Mr Nichols
Sales Manager
Grant & Sons Ltd

Dear Mr Nichols

I would be grateful to receive permission to be absent from work next week (8–12th July).

I am needed to look after my invalid mother. The person who normally looks after her is required urgently elsewhere next week and I have been unable to arrange alternative care. This is an exceptional situation, which I do not anticipate will recur.

I hope that you will give my request sympathetic consideration. I appreciate that I would not be paid for the week.

Yours sincerely

Jane Ryman

---

111 Asking for unpaid leave (other)

(department and date)

Mr R Buick
Financial Director
Croftdown Ltd

Dear Mr Buick

I write to ask if you would please allow me to take one week's unpaid leave, 15–22nd November.

Greyfriars College has written to ask me whether I would like to take advantage of a vacancy on their Extended French course, produced by a cancellation. I have been trying to get on this course for over two years and I know I shall be able to make good use, in my work, of the knowledge I gain.

Places are so sought-after that, if I turn down this opportunity, it might be several years before I get another chance. Unfortunately, since I could not foresee this unexpected offer, I have already used up my holiday entitlement for this year.

My Department Head, Mrs Carr, approves the idea and has kindly agreed to rearrange activities so that my work commitments are well covered during this period. I hope, therefore, that you will find it possible to grant this request.

Yours sincerely

Jane Brown

112 Asking for holiday entitlement

(department and date)

Mrs F Black
Personnel Manager
Third Floor

Dear Mrs Black

I would like to take two weeks of my holiday entitlement from
6–19th June inclusive, and the other two weeks from 9–22nd
September inclusive.

I hope this is convenient.

Yours sincerely

Alan Jones

113 Asking for promotion

(department and date)

Ms K Tope
Accounts Manager
Smith & Co. Ltd

Dear Ms Tope

I write to ask whether you would consider promoting me to the
position of Senior Clerk when Mr John Brown retires later this year.

As you know, I have been working for the Company for four
years, one year as Junior Clerk and three years as Clerk.

I have undertaken the work of a Senior Clerk during periods of
holiday and sickness and, apart from finding the work very
interesting, I believe that I have performed it very satisfactorily.

I would be grateful for the opportunity to discuss this matter with you.

Yours sincerely

Barbara Potter

Where letters are sent through an internal company post, you will only need to put your address within the company, e.g. Department A1. Similarly, the addressee's name, position or department and the name of the company, will be sufficient.

If you do not wish the letter to be seen by anyone other than the addressee, put 'Private' or 'Personal' in the top-left hand corner of the envelope.

---

114 Apology for absence

(address and date)

Miss R Burton
Manageress
Berkely Stores
Church Street
London EC4 8ZZ

Dear Miss Burton

I am so sorry that I did not return to work as expected last Thursday.

Unfortunately, my flight home was held up by the Air Controllers' strike and I did not get home until after the Stores closed on Friday. I reported for work at the normal time on Saturday.

I apologise for the inconvenience my absence caused.

Yours sincerely

Marian Cooper

---

115 Asking for a season ticket loan

(department and date)

J Smith Esq.
Financial Director
Mace and Pole Limited

Dear Mr Smith

As you know, my journey into work is rather long and since the
latest fares increase it is more costly than ever. Considerable
savings can be made by purchasing an annual season ticket, and I
wondered whether it would be possible for Mace and Pole to
advance me the money to purchase one. The repayments could
perhaps be deducted from my salary each month.

I would be most grateful if such an arrangement could be made.

Yours sincerely

Michael Firth

116 Confirming an arrangement for flexible working hours

(department and date)

Mrs M Jones
Personnel Officer
Third Floor

Dear Mrs Jones

Thank you so much for allowing me to talk to you about my
problems, yesterday, and for your kind suggestions.

I have now thought things through and confirm that I will be very
willing to try the flexi-time working that you offered. Starting at
10 am will allow me to get my daughter to school and my elderly

mother up and about. The later finishing time will be no problem since my husband will be home from work to look after them.

I have, at home, my own word processor which is compatible with those used in the office. If there is an emergency at home and I have to leave early, I would be more than happy to complete any work I have outstanding, during the evenings or weekends.

Yours sincerely

Annette Hobbs

---

117 Criticism of canteen food

(department and date)

Mr T Smith
Personnel Manager

Dear Mr Smith

I wish to draw to your attention to the reduction in the standard of food provided by the Company's canteen.

I very much appreciated the well-prepared food which used to be available in the canteen. However, in the middle of March the choice of dishes was cut from four to two, and there was a marked deterioration in quality. I have tried the canteen periodically since then and have always been served over-cooked, luke-warm food. The sharp decline in the number of staff using the canteen suggests to me that my criticisms are widely held.

I would be grateful if you could explain to me how this decline in standards has occurred, and if the Company intends to take steps to improve the situation.

Yours sincerely

Colin Rose

118 Enquiry about toilet facilities

(date)

Ms D Kenny
Personnel Manager
Fifth Floor

Dear Ms Kenny

I wish to draw your attention to the fact that the ladies' toilet facilities on the third floor will be inadequate when the Typing Pool is relocated to this floor in September.

There are only two cubicles and two sinks at present – insufficient for more than 30 members of staff.

Even if this is within the requirements of the Office Regulations, I feel that much work time will be lost if ladies have to queue or climb up to the fourth floor several times a day.

We are all very concerned about this and would be grateful if you would advise us of any plans that are in hand to forestall the problem.

Yours sincerely
On behalf of the Accounts Department

Jean Harris

When you sign any letter on behalf of others, do make absolutely sure they have all *all* seen and agreed to the letter before you send it. If the subject of the letter is a vital and/or controversial one, it would be wise to get them to sign their agreement on a copy of the letter to be retained by you.

119 To a Citizens' Advice Bureau, asking about minimum wage regulations

(address and date)

Citizens' Advice Bureau
30 The Highway
Barford
Beds BF9 3XX

Dear Sirs

I wish to find information about the regulations for minimum wages for Farm Workers and would appreciate anything you could send to me and any advice you can give.

I am 23 years of age and, for the past six months have been employed by Bloggs Farm as a full time Farm Worker. The hours are long, the wages low, and no food or accommodation is provided. I have asked for, but never received, a contract of employment.

Recently, I have found that other workers, sharing the same work, are paid considerably more than I am.

I enjoy my job and would not wish to risk losing it by raising the matter of minimum wages with my employer unless I have the full information to back me. I must say that I believe my employer is as uninformed on the regulations as I am.

I hope you will be able to help me, please. I enclose a postage stamp for your reply.

Yours faithfully

Graham Sproggs

Legislation for such as contracts, minimum wages, etc. is subject to change. Your local Citizens' Advice Bureau should be able to advise you.

120 To a Citizens' Advice Bureau, asking about maternity leave regulations

(address and date)

Citizens' Advice Bureau
17 High Street
Soundwich
Kent AB9 7AA

Dear Sirs

<u>Maternity Leave Regulations</u>

Will you please advise me on the above.

I am single, aged 30, and for the last three years have worked as a waitress at the Wizzy Wine Bar. I am three months pregnant. I have not yet informed my employer because I am afraid that I shall lose my job if I do.

Could you please let me know what protection I have from present regulations. Any advice would be appreciated.

I'm sorry that I cannot call at your offices easily because of the hours that I work.

Yours faithfully

Patricia Blunt

If you cannot find out about employment regulations from your Union or your Trade/Professional Association, the local Citizens' Advice Bureau may be able to guide you and, if necessary, tell you how you can get legal advice.

16

Complaining

When you write a letter of complaint, you should always be quite clear in your mind what response you are seeking. You may be hoping for an apology, some information, action or redress. Make it clear in your letter what you are seeking.

If your letter is just a moan or a means to vent your anger, think twice, and then think again, before you post it. If you get a reply to such a letter, it is not likely that the reply will have solved anything – and may, indeed make you feel more depressed or angry than before!

We say again, never threaten in your letter. Always try to be polite and be as brief and to the point as you can. And, should you want to write anything that could possibly be construed as libellous or defamatory, be very careful. At the very least precede any such comment by 'In my opinion'.

---

121 To a neighbour, about smoke

(address and date)

Dear Mr and Mrs Hinks

I would be grateful if you could speak to your gardener about his bonfires.

The lower end of my small garden abuts your property for about 30 feet. Unfortunately, it is just behind my fence that he has chosen to site his fires. Not only is my garden filled with smoke almost every day, but I am kept awake by the fear of sparks from the unattended bonfire igniting my house.

I tried reasoning with your gardener over the fence, but all he would say was "I've got to get rid of all this rubbish!"

Since your house is so far from my boundary, I'm sure you are not aware of the problem and would wish to put matters right.

Yours sincerely

Mary Green (Mrs)

---

122 To a headmistress, about noisy teenagers

(address and date)

Ms A Courtly
Headmistress
St Adolph's School
Brinkley Road
Brinkley
Leicester LR8 8YY

Dear Ms Courtly

A senior citizen living just down the road from your school seeks your help, please, on a matter that is causing her great distress.

Every afternoon, after school, a group of a dozen or so teenagers gathers on the pavement near my front gate. The problem is that some of the girls spend the whole time – sometimes as much as an hour – emitting ear-splitting screams and shrieks. Apart from this being nerve shattering, I have the dread that, should a girl be attacked or hurt, and be screaming for help, none of us would realise that there was an emergency.

I have tried speaking to the girls but have been greeted by puzzled looks or cheeky replies. I'm sure they do not realise the distress they cause and wonder if you would consider raising the matter with your teenage girls. It's lovely to see young people enjoying life, but I would appreciate it if they could do this without the squeals.

Yours sincerely

Betty MacDonald

If all else fails, problems such as smoke pollution, persistently noisy neighbours, dogs, etc. can be referred to your Environmental Health Officer.

---

123 To The Environmental Health Officer, about unreasonable noise

(address and date)

The Environmental Health Officer
Copley Borough Council
Municipal Buildings
High Street
Copley
Sussex BN3 4PP

Dear Sir

Unreasonable noise

I wish to complain about the early start being made by builders working on the flats in Spellthorne Park Road, which is only a few metres from our back garden.

For the last few days, work has commenced as early as 5 am! Since they are stacking and laying bricks, you can imagine the noise. Surely such an early start cannot be permitted, for it is almost impossible to sleep once they have begun.

Since, I understand, the work is likely to continue for some weeks, I would be most grateful if you could look into this matter as soon as possible, to ensure that work begins at a more reasonable time.

Yours faithfully

S J Carter

---

124 Reporting a dangerous road crossing to the Council

(address and date)

The Highways Department
Mossley Council
19–41 High Road
Mossley
Essex EX5 9SR

Dear Sirs

Hazardous road crossing

I wish to draw your attention to the pedestrian crossing on Blanks Road, about 30 metres north of Blanks Avenue. In my opinion, this crossing is a hazard.

Its siting, just over the brow of a hill, means that northbound traffic has insufficient warning of the crossing. The danger is increased after dark because overhanging trees virtually obliterate the light from the crossing beacons and surrounding lamp posts.

I drive along this stretch of road at least twice a day and have frequently witnessed narrowly averted accidents. I urge you to act promptly before a serious accident occurs.

I feel the crossing should be resited. Warning signs before the crossing would help, but I feel they would not eliminate the danger. In any event, the overhanging trees should be cut back immediately.

Please let me know as soon as possible what action you propose to take.

Yours faithfully

Anne Waters (Ms)

---

125 To a builder, complaining about work carried out

(address and date)

Your ref. SB 197/bv

Mr B Vickers
Manager
Stone & Brix (Builders) Ltd
Rise Road
Riseton
Lancs LN6 4PQ

Dear Mr Vickers

Your builders recently carried out some structural alterations and redecoration at my house. You will recall that I phoned you on June 6th and June 21st to complain that some of the work is most unsatisfactory. You promised to send round your inspector, but he has not called.

Confirming what I told you on the phone: large cracks have appeared in the new plasterwork on the ceiling in the lounge extension; the door from the garden to this extension is out of alignment and cannot be locked; the extension windows are both stuck fast and cannot be opened.

I believe that the ceiling could be in a dangerous state and I have, therefore, forbidden my family to go into the extension room. However, with the door unlockable, someone could enter from the garden.

Will you, or your inspector, examine the problems immediately, please, before someone gets injured. Otherwise, I shall be compelled to seek the advice of your Building Federation – and this I would prefer not to do, since you have always done such excellent work for us, and for our friends and neighbours, in the past.

Yours sincerely

Timothy Weston

---

126 To a manufacturer, complaining about repairs to a washing machine

(Address and date)

Your ref. AWMC/3001/D

The Service Manager
Electronwash Ltd
Kings House
Gorfordtown
Lincs LA3 6ZQ

Dear Sir

Automatic Washing Machine: Electronwash Z/9000567N

I wish to complain about the repairs made to my machine, under guarantee, and to receive your explanation.

I purchased the machine from Rowtleys of Gorbridge on 3rd July 199- and it was installed on 6th July.

I tried a load of washing on 7th July but, to my horror, the washing cycle continued on and on and, after two hours, I had to switch off at the mains and bale out the machine. I immediately phoned your Service Hotline. The young lady was very sympathetic and said that one of your engineers would inspect the machine at 10 am the next day.

I took a half day of my leave entitlement to be at home. Engineer A arrived on time, checked the machine, said it needed a new printed circuit board, ordered it on his portable computer system, and said he would fix it on 12th July.

I was forced to take another half day's leave. On time, Engineer B arrived. He inspected the machine, said the fault had been wrongly diagnosed by Engineer A, changed around some wiring, and left.

To cut a long story short, this time the machine would not fill with water, your Hotline agreed to send back Engineer A (with the circuit board) on 14th July, another half day's leave! Engineer A spent three hours locating and reinstating the wiring changes made by Engineer B, and ten minutes changing the circuit board. When I commented that Engineer B was, in my opinion, an expensive menace, Engineer A said he was new to the job and that engineers had to learn, didn't they.

My machine now works perfectly but at the cost of one and a half days' annual leave. For the sake of your firm's good name, I thought I should bring the matter to your attention and ask for an explanation.

Yours faithfully

Stephanie White

With such a letter, you could try asking for compensation, even though you think it unlikely such will be offered. You should, at least, get a full apology, and the firm should take action that ensures such incidents do not reoccur.

127 Concerning goods not complying with the Sale of Goods Act

(address and date)

The Manager
Comfort Home Furniture
51–53 High Road
Fairford
Essex ES9 7ES

Dear Sir

Purchase receipt No. R635

I bought a sofa (Highfield, No. 87, Kingfisher) from your shop six months ago, on 2nd April. Although it has not received more than normal use, it collapsed yesterday.

It seems, from a cursory inspection, that the frame has broken near to a section where some repair work had previously been carried out, presumably during manufacture.

The sofa, when purchased, was, therefore, not of merchantable quality under the terms of the Sale of Goods Act.

Will you please arrange for the sofa to be removed and for a refund of the full purchase price, as a matter of urgency.

Yours faithfully

David Miles

128 To a credit card company, concerning a fraudulent overcharge

(address and date)

The Managing Director
CroupCard Ltd
Ashley Buildings
Crumpster
Notts NJ9 9XX

Dear Sir

Card Number CCL 1234 5678 9011 – Charles Purbrook

I have just received your statement dated 14 April 199-. The item dated 6th March 199-, Buggins Garage, Mobrook, for £17.85 is an overcharge. The amount should, correctly, be £7.85.

I attach a photocopy of the sales receipt. I can only assume that someone fraudulently changed the 7 to 17, that is, the SEVEN to SEVENTEEN.

You will further note that the sale is detailed as for petrol. Since my car is a Mini, I could not possibly have got £17.85 worth of petrol into the tank, even when absolutely empty.

Will you please send me a corrected statement immediately, so that I do not incur charges for late payment.

Yours faithfully

Charles Purbrook

Enc.

129 To a tour operator, about a spoiled holiday

(address and date)

The Managing Director
Sandy Tours Ltd
149 Regency Lanes
London EW6 9AB

Dear Sir

<u>Holiday No. 67, Mediterranean Beaches, 2nd – 9th July 199-</u>
<u>Mr and Mrs Tom Brown, Booking reference: STMB/7/38/9</u>

I wish to complain, strongly, about the last minute changes made
to our holiday by your Tour Representative in Sunbella.

We booked the seven day holiday with your company because
we wanted seven days on the beach at Sunbella. At the end of
the fourth day, we were called to a meeting by your
Representative and told that we would be spending the last two
nights in a hotel in the heart of the town of Centresville. Most of
us protested angrily, but your Representative was adamant. I
tried to phone your London office, but was told nothing could be
done.

The fifth day was wasted as members of the tour held a meeting
and did some 'detective' work. It emerged that only four of the
forty tour members wanted to go to Centresville and had, indeed,
requested this 'for shopping'! This was accepted by your
Representative, without asking the rest of us. The hotel at
Sunbella had already arranged for a party from, I think, Japan, to
take our rooms. Thirty-six out of the forty tour members signed a
formal complaint, which we gave to your Representative.

Our two nights in Centresville were utterly wretched. The hotel
was pleasant enough, but the noise and the heat were unbearable.
And, had we wanted a 'town' holiday, we would have booked a
'town holiday'.

I now ask for a reasonable, proportionate, refund for the two
days ruined, the inconvenience and distress, and the out-of-
pocket costs, for my wife and me. We are in touch with other

members of the tour, who, we understand, will also be writing to you.

Yours faithfully

Tom and Sheila Brown

---

130 To a Citizens' Advice Bureau, about unfair eviction from rented property

(address and date)

Citizens' Advice Bureau
Stanley Court
Chapel Road
Blessop
Lincs LA77 9QQ

Dear Sirs

I am having problems with my landlord and seek your advice, please, on my legal position.

I have been renting a partly-furnished two-bedroom flat at the above address for just over five years, during which time I have never been in arrears with the rent which, now, is £65 per week.

I have looked after the place well and have even carried out repairs myself, rather than troubling my landlord.

On 16th August, my landlord told me that he needed my flat for his brother-in-law's use, and gave me notice to leave by 15th September. When I protested, he said there is nothing I can do except leave, and that decorators will be arriving on 16th September to prepare the flat for his brother-in-law.

I hope you will be able to advise me, please, since I have no idea to whom I can turn for help.

Yours faithfully

George Hamilcar

Landlord and tenant regulations are subject to change. As things stand at the time of writing, you should seek guidance and information from a Citizens' Advice Bureau *before* making any approach to an official body such as The Rent Officer, The Rent Assessment Committee or The Rent Tribunal, on any land-lord/tenant problem.

---

131 To your MP, about a local problem

(address and date)

Stephen Langthwaite Esq. MBE MP
House of Commons
London SW1A 0AA

Dear Mr Langthwaite

Portshire County Council's plans for Pilchester Village

Pilchester needs your support – before it is too late and our village suffers an irreversible fate in the name of Council 'progress'. Please will you help your constituents?

We understand that plans are well in hand for the meadows at the end of the High Street (Green Belt) to be developed as a Swimming Pool complex.

We do not believe that this is an appropriate site and we also question if public money should be used for such a development.

Traffic to the complex would have to negotiate our very narrow High Street. This is, already, full of pot-holes and – despite many pleas to the Council – no repairs have been made in the last three years. The excuse given is always the lack of Council funds. Similarly, and for the same excuse, we have no pedestrian crossing in the village.

Our group, The Friends of Pilchester Village, has the active support of 200 villagers – well over half of the community. Any support that you can give us would be much appreciated.

Yours sincerely

Emily Forbes-Long

Secretary
The Friends of Pilchester Village

Index of Sample Letters

LOVE AND MARRIAGE

CLUBS AND SOCIETIES

ILLNESS AND DEATH

MONEY MATTERS

DOMESTIC MATTERS

AT WORK

COMPLAINING